High praise for the English edition of
Channels of Healing Prayer:

"A beautiful little book."
> **John Kearns**
> *The Catholic Herald*

"This book...will have wide appeal. It clearly merits particular interest among health care professionals and all who are actively involved in The Christian Healing Ministry."
> **Dr. Clare Whitehead,**
> Rehabilitation Specialist
> in *Way of Life*

"...an excellent overall picture of the use of prayer for healing."
> *Burrswood Herald*

"Benedict Heron has written an important book....He writes with confidence and great care."
> *The Tablet* (London)

"I give thanks for the wisdom, clarity, honesty and warm encouragement to be found in this book. I find it greatly refreshing."
> **Bernice Joachim** in
> *Towards Wholeness*

Channels of Healing Prayer

Benedict Heron

Foreword by Francis MacNutt

AVE MARIA PRESS
Notre Dame, Indiana 46556

This book is dedicated to the many kind people
who have supported the writing of it with their prayers.
Without their prayers it would
certainly never have been written.

Scripture quotations are mainly from the Revised Standard Version
Common Bible, copyright 1973 by the Division of Christian Education of
the National Council of Churches of Christ in the USA. Used by permission.

First published in 1989 as *Praying for Healing: The Challenge* by Darton,
Longman and Todd, Ltd. 89 Lillie Road, London SW6 1UD.

International Standard Book Number: 0-87793-484-3
Library of Congress Catalog Card Number: 92-71594

Cover design by Elizabeth J. French

Printed and bound in the United States of America

July 1992

Contents

Acknowledgements

It is customary for authors to thank publishers. However, in this case there are very special reasons for doing so. The idea of this book was born when Morag Reeve and Teresa de Bertodano of DLT visited our monastery and invited me to write a book on healing, insisting that I could and should write this book in the face of my hesitations and very serious doubts. Morag Reeve continued to encourage warmly and to help me throughout the period of writing. So this book very much owes its existence to the initiative of the publishers.

Special thanks must also be given to Jill Oakey, who generously typed the manuscript, deciphering my difficult scribble and making valuable suggestions. Thanks also to Jacquie Fox-Little for secretarial help in connection with the book.

Thanks are also due to three people who read through the manuscript and made helpful comments and suggestions: my colleague, Fr Mark M. Schrum OSB, Fr Hubert Condron CP and Eileen Shaughnessy. Furthermore, special thanks are due to the two medical doctors, Joseph and Dorothy Briffa, who generously looked after the healing testimonies at the end of the book. Without their help, I could not have coped with that side of the book. Thanks also to the people who kindly shared the testimony of their healing.

Finally, I must thank our monks and nuns in Turvey and my sister, Joanna Wates, who kindly provided peaceful refuges to which I could go in order to get on with the writing. And thanks to my monastic brethren in Cockfosters for their encouragement and support.

BENEDICT M. HERON OSB

11 November 1988

Foreword

I remember first meeting Fr. Benedict Heron at a national Catholic charismatic conference in England in 1975, when charismatic renewal was still fresh and new—and growing at an astounding rate. Since then the growth has slowed for a variety of reasons, but I trust its main lessons remain very much with us. The healing ministry, in particular, stays with us, and praying for healing, which was a startling innovation in 1967, has now become established in many parts of the Catholic world. The renewal is now older and perhaps wiser. Hopefully, its first fervor has not just gotten chilled with age.

Clearly, Fr. Heron has not lost the excitement of his first discovery of the healing ministry. As an older priest—and as an Englishman—the enthusiasm reflected in these pages is a quiet enthusiasm, but very real. When Fr. Heron speaks about clergy who don't seem to understand that now, since Vatican II, the sacrament of anointing the sick is meant to be used for anointing any sick person who is seriously ill, he confessed to being "deeply saddened"; but then he realizes that his disappointment runs deeper than that and that he really feels "angry" at the situation (p. 26), more than twenty-five years after the council has ended. Benedict is a fine example of an older priest who has maintained his youthful excitement about the things of God, combined with mature wisdom and an openness to learning from experience.

At that conference in Hopwood Hall, I remember his coming up to me and asking if we could set aside a time to pray for his long-standing depression, for which he was then receiving treatment. Since several hundred people crowded the conference, we were still looking to set aside a time when he decided to come up in a healing line after mass to receive a relatively brief prayer. I can still recall how he then quietly rested on the chapel floor for more than two hours.

Naturally we were curious afterward to find out what was happening during those hours, so he shared how the Lord had taken him through his entire life and showed him people whom he had forgotten but whom he still needed to forgive. As he writes:

> I also learned more about the nature and demands of Christian forgiveness while lying on the ground there than I had ever understood from talks or books. The Holy Spirit gave me a much deeper insight on this subject, which I regard as one of the major blessings of my life (p. 70).

Talking to him at that time, I felt that God had not only specially blessed him for his own personal spiritual growth, but that God would use him in a special way to bring healing to others.

Indeed, when I returned to England in 1992 and again met Fr. Heron, I found that my hope had certainly come true: not only has he been used to renew the healing ministry in England, but he is widely respected; his own Benedictine community has chosen him as prior of their monastery in North London. Certainly God has joined his natural gift of compassion (sharpened by the pain in his own life) together with his thoughtfulness and practical wisdom, to write an honest, compact testimony that can help any Christian learn about healing. I found it an easy, fascinating book to read—very balanced, truthful, and truly practical. His honesty shines through these pages, and the reader can trust everything Fr. Heron writes as a guide to understanding Christ's tender healing ministry.

Certainly, if I had read a book like this when I was twenty years old, it would have changed my life; I would not have had to wait another twenty years before I discovered how much Jesus still sees the people as "harassed and dejected, like sheep without a shepherd" (Mt 9:3b) and that his answer today as then is to commission his disciples to heal and to proclaim that the kingdom of God is at hand.

I only wish that every Catholic might read this book.

FRANCIS S. MACNUTT
Director, Christian Healing Ministries
Jacksonville, Florida
10 April 1992

Introduction

It was seventeen years ago in 1972 when I first came across the ministry of Christian prayer for healing in the Charismatic Renewal. This marked a turning point in my life as a Christian and as a priest. At the time I was suffering from depression, and the present and future looked very bleak. Prayer for healing not only brought hope to me, but I found that through the ministry of healing prayer I was used to bring hope and healing to others. It would be nice to be able to say that my depression, fears and anxieties disappeared overnight, and that as soon as I began to lay hands on the blind they saw. But that is not what happened to me, although some people have had that kind of experience. Mine has been the path of a gradual continuing healing for myself and a gradual growth of my healing ministry for others – and the progress continues.

Not that I have never experienced immediate healing. About thirteen years ago the cartilage in my right knee went. I was limping badly, and I could only walk downstairs by putting my right foot first. My knee was X-rayed in the hospital and the consultant said that an operation was necessary, so we fixed the date. A few weeks later an Anglican priest with a powerful ministry of healing, Colin Urquhart, laid hands on my knee and prayed. I had limped into his church, I ran when I got outside it. I walked up and down the stairs normally when I returned to the monastery. The hospital physiotherapist was astounded when she saw me the next day because I was not limping in the same way; the operation was cancelled, and I have never had to consult a doctor about my knee since then. So I know from personal experience what it is to receive an immediate healing from the Lord Jesus. However, the most important healings I have received, including physical healing, have been gradual, and that is normally how healing takes place in answer to prayer.

Having experienced the healing touch of the Lord myself, and having been used to bring his healing touch to others – at a modest level – I feel a burning desire to spread to others the good news that Jesus still heals today in answer to prayer. I have met many people who have received more important healing in answer to prayer than I have – I think of Ernest who the doctors said would die from cancer before last Christmas and is now free from cancer; I think of Vera who was (and still is) registered as blind, and who can now tell the time on her wrist-watch in the normal way, and who also received a very extraordinary healing of her back; I think of Sister Eleanor, who was dying from bronchiectasis, a sickness of the lungs, and who now rides a bicycle and leads the singing; I think of Margaret whose back condition was really desperate and dangerous, and who now travels about normally; I think of George who is no longer suicidal and who now copes with his job normally. I have also met many Christians from different churches who certainly have much more powerful healing ministries than I have. So what I am writing about in this book is not primarily my experience of being healed and being used to heal, but about the wider renewal of the healing ministry as I have seen it and experienced it, primarily in the Charismatic Renewal but also outside this renewal where God is also raising up healing ministries. So I am largely writing on behalf of others who may not have the time or the ability to write themselves but who are often more powerfully involved in the healing ministry than I am. I am writing about a collective experience of a growing number of people who have received healing through Christian prayer and/or have been used by Jesus to heal others through prayer.

Prayer for healing is primarily concerned with helping needy people – which is all of us in one way or another. Our main motive in praying for healing must be love for needy people, the desire to try to bring Jesus' healing love to someone or some group of people. However, the renewal of the healing ministry is not only important for the individuals prayed for. It is important also for the strengthening of the faith of Christians in general, and for the spread of the gospel. Jesus said to his disciples: 'You shall receive power when the Holy Spirit has come upon you; and you shall be my witnesses in Jerusalem and in all Judea and Samaria and to the end of the earth' (Acts 1:8). Many people do not see much spiritual power in most of our Christian congregations, so they wonder whether Christianity is really anything more than words. When the loving power of Jesus is seen in healings, then people will believe or believe more strongly in the Jesus who heals and in the Heavenly Father who sent him.

This book is written in the first place for Roman Catholics, although it is hoped that other Christians will also find it helpful. In recent years there have been so many good books on the Christian healing ministry of prayer by Anglicans and Christians of the reformed tradition and so few by Roman Catholics, at least on this side of the Atlantic, that it seems justifiable to write primarily for Catholics.

The problems connected with the renewal of the healing ministry in the Catholic Church are somewhat different to those in other churches. Traditionally Catholics have always believed in healing miracles. However, they usually do not expect them to happen in their own lives or in their parishes. Catholics need to believe that Jesus wants to heal in their parish, in their family. Not that Jesus wants to heal everyone physically in this life, but that he wants everyone to experience his healing touch in one way or another – and we need to remember that spiritual healing is always the most important area of healing – and we all need spiritual healing.

I hope this book will be a real challenge to people, a challenge to pray for healing, a challenge to see whether the living Jesus still heals today. What is needed in the church now, I think, is not primarily a very few people with great gifts of healing – although I am sure God wants to give an increasing number of people great gifts of healing. I think what is especially needed is to spread the ministry of healing, to encourage Christians in every congregation to pray for healing, to raise up ministries of healing in every parish.

May this book be used by the Holy Spirit to forward this renewal of the healing ministry in the Church.

1

Healing in the New Testament

Jesus was clearly by far the greatest healer of all times. No other founder of a religion comes anywhere near him in this field. Jesus was and remains a unique inspirer and example as a healer.

Nearly one-fifth of the four Gospels is devoted to Jesus' healing ministry and discussions connected with it. This shows both how much of his public ministry was devoted to healing and how important this ministry was in the eyes of the four evangelists. Try to imagine what the Gospels would be like if all reference to Jesus' healing miracles were not there. The Gospels truncated in this way would simply not make sense. The crowds would not have gathered in such great numbers as they did to hear Jesus preach and teach if there had been no signs and wonders to confirm the message. And the miracles added authority to his teaching: 'And they were astonished at his teaching, for he taught them as one who had authority, and not as the scribes' (Mark 1:22).

What would have been the first thing that an ordinary Jew living in Galilee at the time of Jesus would have heard about him? It would not usually have been his teaching that first of all attracted attention, but rather the healing miracles. People would probably have gone to him in the first place to be healed, or to take their family or friends to be healed, or to see people healed.

And when they got out of the boat, immediately the people recognized him, and ran about the whole neighbourhood and began to bring sick people on their palletts to any place where they heard he was. And wherever he came, in villages, cities, or country, they laid the sick in the market places, and besought him that they might touch even the fringe of his garment; and as many as touched it were made well. (Mark 6:54–6)

Just imagine that in Hyde Park today someone was in one afternoon restoring sight to several blind people, healing people on stretchers and in wheelchairs, so that they got up and walked, praying for cancer cases so that the tumours disappeared. Police reinforcements and extra buses would be needed for the vast crowds! Indeed, special charter planes would be laid on!

The first impression that Jesus would have made on most people would surely have been that of an infinitely loving, compassionate man who cared very deeply for the sick and suffering and who was able to help and heal them. And this would have made an even deeper impression in an age when there was no modern medicine, no National Health Service and no social security. 'As he went ashore he saw a great throng; and he had compassion on them, and healed their sick' (Matthew 14:14).

Most people surely first became interested in the preaching and teaching of Jesus because he was the great healer. Obviously everyone would be especially interested to hear what a great miracle worker had to say about life, about religion, about the problems of society. Much of the teaching in the Sermon on the Mount must have been hard for many Jews to accept, for example: 'But I say to you, Love your enemies and pray for those who persecute you' (Matthew 5:44) (cf. Matthew 5:10–12). Jesus' visible love and compassion and the miracles must have helped to pave the way for the acceptance of his teaching.

The healing miracles of Jesus must have created a highly emotional atmosphere. Tears of joy must have been flowing as people found they could walk again, as people saw their relatives and friends healed, as the crowd witnessed the healing of the blind. In healing services today we sometimes see tears flowing when people receive the healing touch of the Lord. How much more must tears have flowed and hearts been touched when Jesus was healing the sick in Galilee! 'And great crowds came to him, bringing with them the lame, the maimed, the blind, the dumb, and many others, and they put them at his feet, and he healed them, so that the throng wondered, when they saw the dumb speaking, the maimed whole, the lame walking, and the blind seeing; and they glorified the God of Israel' (Matthew 15:30–1).

Today when many Christians are too suspicious and frightened of the emotions it is good to remind ourselves that life with Jesus must have been at times extremely emotional for the disciples. Indeed they must have emotionally plumbed the heights and the depths, ending up with Calvary followed by the Resurrection.

Furthermore, the memory of being healed by Jesus or seeing other people healed by him is not something which would have disappeared with time. For many people being healed by Jesus must have remained the great event of their lives, something never to be forgotten, something ever to be grateful for, something which transformed their lives. And it is not as though Jesus only performed a few healing miracles. 'That evening they brought to him many who were possessed with demons; and he cast out the spirits with a word, and healed all who were sick' (Matthew 8:16). That was just one evening! Thus we must surely reckon that many thousands of people in Israel had been healed by Jesus, or seen people healed by him, or known people healed by him.

All this is surely very different from the more formal and unemotional atmosphere in which many Christians feel at home today. They would tend to think that when searching for the truth the emotions need to be kept out of the way; they would perhaps suggest that signs and wonders should be kept out of intellectual discussions. Indeed, they would often thoroughly disapprove of a Christian meeting which began to resemble the emotional gatherings round Jesus in Galilee. Did Jesus get it wrong in performing miracles and touching the emotions? Or did the evangelists get it wrong by giving us a false picture of Jesus and his ministry? Or have many sophisticated Christians of the Western World sometimes got it wrong when they are frightened or wary of healing miracles and the stirring of the emotions? Obviously there can be false claims of miracles and emotionalism of the wrong kind. But if the New Testament remains the basic reference point for all future generations, then surely every Christian community should be open to healing miracles and the touching of the emotions.

Jesus during his public ministry went about healing the sick and casting out demons. He regarded sickness as an evil to be combatted. 'And he stood over her and rebuked the fever and it left her' (Luke 4:39). Indeed he sometimes healed people by casting out demons (cf. Matthew 9:32), and he referred to the woman 'bent over' as having 'a spirit of infirmity for eighteen years' and as 'a daughter of Abraham whom Satan bound for eighteen years' (Luke 13:11). Nowhere is it suggested in the Gospels that Jesus welcomed sickness, or regarded it as something good, or referred to it as sent by God. This would appear to be in marked contrast to those Christians today who start by regarding sickness as a blessing sent by God, to be simply accepted and indeed welcomed. The fact that God brings good out of evil if we let him, that he sometimes brings much good out of sickness, does not mean that disease is not in itself and in general an evil. In heaven there will be no sickness!

Jesus healed people in the first place because he loved them, had compassion for them, had pity on them. 'And a leper came to him beseeching him, and kneeling said to him, "If you will you can make me clean". Moved with pity, he stretched out his hand and touched him, and said to him, "I will, be clean" ' (Mark 1:40). However Jesus' healing miracles were also a sign of who he was, the Anointed One of God. Although at times Jesus asked people he had healed not to publicize the healings (cf. Mark 7:36), he nevertheless referred to the healing miracles as reasons for believing in him and his message: 'The works that I do in my Father's name, they bear witness to me' (John

10:25); 'Believe me that I am in the Father and the Father in me; or else believe me for the sake of the works themselves' (John 14:11).

Jesus not only healed the sick himself. He commanded his disciples to heal in his name: 'And he called the twelve together and gave them power and authority over all demons and to cure diseases, and he sent them out to preach the kingdom of God and to heal. . . . And they departed and went through the villages, preaching the gospel and healing everywhere' (Luke 9) (cf. Luke 10:9 for the seventy). Jesus also promised that 'these signs will accompany those who believe: in my name they will cast out demons . . . they will lay their hands on the sick, and they will recover' (Mark 16:17).

This is what we see happening when we read the history of the New Testament church in the Bible, especially in the Acts of the Apostles: they preached the Kingdom of God and healed the sick in the name of Jesus. 'And they went forth and preached everywhere, while the Lord worked with them and confirmed the message by the signs that attended it. Amen' (Mark 16:20).

Clearly the healing miracles played a key part in the spreading of the gospel. The disciples proclaimed the gospel, said that Jesus had risen from the dead. Then in the name of Jesus they healed people and it was surely then or especially then that people began to believe. Take, for example, the healing of the man born lame in Acts 3. The man is healed, the Jews are amazed and wonder how it happened, Peter says that the man was healed in the name of Jesus and proclaims the gospel, and many of those who heard the word believed; and the number of men came to about five thousand (Acts 4:4). The conversion of the five thousand was obviously directly linked with the man born lame.

The disciples themselves clearly expected healing miracles to follow the preaching of the gospel, as we see in their prayer after the release of Peter and John: 'And now, Lord, look upon their threats, and grant to thy servants to speak the word with all boldness, while thou stretchest out thy hand to heal, and signs and wonders are performed through the name of thy servant Jesus' (Acts 4:29).

Paul also realized that healing miracles were a part of his ministry as an apostle. Writing to the Corinthians defending his ministry as an apostle, he says: 'The signs of a true apostle were performed among you in all patience, with signs and wonders and mighty works' (2 Corinthians 12:12). The Acts of the Apostles gives a number of examples of healing miracles linked with Paul, even to the point that 'God did extraordinary miracles by the hands of Paul, so that handkerchiefs or aprons were carried away from his body to the sick, and diseases left them and the evil spirits came out of them' (Acts 19:11). Furthermore, Paul recognized that gifts of healing would normally be given to some people in the local church. Writing to the Corinthians he includes 'gifts of healings' and the 'gift of working miracles' in his list of gifts of the Spirit (cf. 1 Corinthians 12).

In the Letter of James we find the text which is the main biblical basis for the Sacrament of the Anointing of the Sick:

> Is any among you sick? Let him call for the elders of the church, and let them pray over him, anointing him with oil in the name of the Lord; and the prayer of faith will save the sick man, and the Lord will raise him up; and if he has committed sins, he will be forgiven. Therefore confess your sins to one another, and pray for one another, that you may be healed. The prayer of the righteous man has great power in its effects. (James 5:14–16)

Here reference is made not to people with special gifts of healing as in 1 Corinthians 12, but to 'the elders of the church'. So it would seem that there were different levels of ministry to the sick. There were Christians who had special gifts of healings and there were others who prayed for the sick because they were elders in the Christian community – although of course some of the elders may also have had charismatic gifts of healings.

It would be a mistake of course to think that no one in the New Testament church was ever ill, or that people were always healed or healed immediately in answer to prayer. Timothy was advised to 'no longer drink only water, but use a little wine for the sake of your stomach and your frequent ailments' (1 Timothy 5:23). So Timothy had 'frequent ailments' which were not simply banished by prayer. Trophimus was 'left ill at Miletus' (2 Timothy 4:20). Paul wrote to the Galatians: 'You know it was because of a bodily ailment that I preached the gospel to you at first; and though my condition was a trial to you, you did not scorn or despise me' (4:13). So there is no warrant in the New Testament for the view that a Christian should never be ill! Nor is there New Testament backing for the view that Christians should never use medical remedies, for the oil and wine mentioned above were seen as such in those days.

Life of course was far from easy in the New Testament church, for they had to face persecution of one kind or another. However, the miracles, which were mainly connected with healings, must have helped to bring joy and increase of faith. It must have been very exciting seeing a cripple getting up and walking. (Imagine that the blind were receiving their sight at Sunday morning Mass! The young would no longer complain of boredom and cease coming. The problem of dwindling congregations would vanish. Even parish finance would recover!)

Not a few Christians today seem to look down on the whole subject of healing miracles and of signs and wonders. They would regard an interest in such things as a sign of immaturity, both human and religious. Such things, they might say, may be alright or necessary for simple uneducated peasants, but they are not for the mature educated Christian at the end of the twentieth century. We should not need such things to enliven our interest and strengthen our faith. Such a view is, I suspect, common in the declining liberal churches. It is of course not found in the growing Pentecostal churches. And this may explain in part why the former are declining and the latter growing.

A Catholic computer expert said to me recently that he had found the sight of a man confined to a wheelchair suddenly getting up and walking at a Protestant healing service a very faith building experience. God chose healing miracles and signs and wonders as a means of building faith in the New Testament church. They are still building faith today in churches and groups which are open to receiving them. Let us not try to be more 'spiritual' or more 'mature' than the New Testament church!

Clearly Pope John Paul II is someone who believes that healing miracles, including those not officially authenticated by the Church, are still very relevant today. It is appropriate to close this chapter with some wise words of the Pope addressed on Saturday 19 November 1988 to a symposium organized by the Congregation for the Causes of the Saints:

> The healings, the extraordinary gifts, are numerous. They are not always known, and even less are they carefully verified in the framework of a serious evaluation and subsequently recognized as authentic by the Church. Yet these signs can be reminders, messages which show that God is Love. They have effected numerous conversions, they have motivated many persons to live a more sincere and generous gift of self, most often unknown to the world. (See the Osservatore Romano, English edition, 19 December 1988)

2

Praying for Healing and the Medical Professions

Treat the doctor with the honour that is his due,
in consideration of his services;
for he too has been created by the Lord.
Healing itself comes from the Most High,
like a gift received from a king.
The doctor's learning keeps his head high,
and the great regard him with awe.
The Lord has brought forth medicinal herbs from the ground,
and no one sensible will despise them.
Did not a piece of wood once sweeten the water,
thus giving proof of its power?
He has also given some people the knowledge,
so that they may draw credit from his mighty works.
He uses these for healing and relieving pain;
the druggist makes up a mixture from them.
Thus, there is no end to his activities;
thanks to him, well-being exists throughout the world.
My child, when you are ill, do not rebel,
but pray to the Lord and he will heal you.
Renounce your faults, keep your hands unsoiled,
and cleanse your heart from all sin.
Offer incense and a memorial of fine flour,
make as rich an offering as you can afford.
Then let the doctor take over – the Lord created him too –
do not let him leave you, for you need him.
There are times when good health depends on doctors.
For they, in their turn, will pray the Lord

to grant them the grace to relieve
and to heal, and so prolong your life.
Whoever sins in the eyes of his Maker,
let such a one come under the care of the doctor!

(Sirach 38:1–15)

This passage from the ancient book of Sirach, for Catholics a
part of the Old Testament, is surely remarkable, for it contains
several fundamental truths about the relationship between sickness, prayer and the medical professions. We are to pray for
healing, we are to honour and make use of those involved in
the field of medicine, and they are to pray for their work to
bring healing. God also heals through the work of the medical
professions and through medicines.

Thank God for doctors, dentists, nurses and other members
of the medical professions. How horrified many of us would
feel if we were informed that henceforth we would have to face
life without being able to see a doctor or a dentist! And what
a sobering thought it is to remember that some of the poor of
this world do more or less face life without them. As I sit in
the dentist's chair, I do thank God for dentists, I do admire
their skill – I myself would have made a most incompetent one.
And I do ask God to bless the dentist's work, including his or
her work on me!

There seem to be basically three different attitudes among
Christians with regard to the relationship between sickness,
prayer and medicine. There are those many Christians who in
fact think that the healing of physical sickness is the work of
the medical professions and not a matter for prayer. There are
secondly a small number of Christians who apparently believe
that all healing should really come through prayer and that
ideally at least Christians should not have to make use of
medical help. Finally, there are the Christians who consider
that we should seek healing both through prayer and through
the help of the medical professions. Let us examine these three

approaches – which doubtless contain variations within each group.

(1) In view of the express command of Jesus to his disciples to pray for the healing of the sick (cf. Luke 9:1 and 10:8; also Mark 16:18) and the example of the New Testament church as seen in the Acts of the Apostles, it is very surprising that so many Christians today think that at least physical healing is only a matter for the medical professions and that praying for healing has no place in our scientific age. It is for me even more surprising to meet clergy who adopt this view.

This approach not only goes against the New Testament, it is also contrary to the tradition of the Church, and it seems to ignore the undoubted fact that many Christians are being healed in answer to prayer in our own times. The result of this approach is that some people die who would have survived if there had been serious prayer for healing, and that some people remain ill who could be healed through prayer.

(2) The attitude that Christians really ought not to need to go to the doctor, that if they had sufficient faith they would be healed through prayer, can lead to major tragedies. People could die who might recover if they received medical attention. Depressed people could commit suicide because they did not receive medication in time. Apparently in the USA a few diabetics die each year because they stop taking insulin after prayer, thinking that if they have enough faith they need not take medication. Needless to say, this approach can do much to bring the healing ministry of prayer into disrepute.

(3) The third approach which believes in both praying for healing and making use of the medical professions, harmonizing the two as the circumstances demand, is the subject of the rest of this chapter. The need to harmonize and to increase the co-operation between the prayer side and the medical side of healing is one of the main tasks of the future. As I write, I remember a case of such co-operation which was truly blessed. A little girl, Natalia, aged nine months, was thought to be dying in the intensive care ward of a London teaching hospital.

The mother of the child asked members of our healing team to go and pray with the child. I remember feeling rather awe-struck as, dressed in a white gown and with a mask on, I prayed over the little child who was sedated. The bed seemed to be largely surrounded with machines connected to the child by tubes. There were several nurses and a doctor in the room. For the next two or three weeks one or other member of our healing team, including a medical doctor, prayed over that child every day. From the first day of our prayers she began to improve, but there were ups and downs, especially when the ventilation side was causing trouble. However she pulled through, and I last saw her as a little girl running around. It would be good to see more cases of co-operation of that kind.

I find myself full of admiration for the dedication and skill of many doctors, nurses and other medical personnel, whether working individually or as members of a team as in the case of Natalia in the intensive care ward. I know a paediatrician who having worked all day quite frequently stays up most of the night trying to save a new-born baby. I know nurses who are working heroically in caring for patients in scandalously understaffed situations in hospitals. I remember the atmosphere of dedicated concentration in an operating theatre during major operations – during the last World War I worked in London hospitals for a time. Let us give credit where credit is due!

However, dedicated medical attention by itself frequently does not seem to be enough. Medically speaking, it is often a mystery why one person gets better and another does not. And prayer for healing can often be part of the answer to that mystery. The turning point for Natalia came when the healing prayer ministry started.

There is a further consideration. Providing increasingly expensive medical care for our ageing population is causing growing financial and practical problems. As we know, suffering people are having to wait for a year or more in many cases for hip or other operations. This situation may well get worse – and, of course, things are far far worse for most people in the Third World. The growth of the healing ministry of prayer will certainly help to relieve the problems of an overburdened National Health Service. I am sure that the prayer ministry of our healing teams has unquestionably saved medical expenditure.

To start with a personal example: I myself have caused the National Health Service little expense for over a decade now. I am sure this is linked with the fact that I pray for my own healing and get others to do so for me, with the result that I rarely have to go to my doctor. Of course I may have a major operation next year, because anybody may have to do so. But I believe it remains true that in general more prayer for healing will help to reduce demands on the over-stretched medical services.

Our prayer for healing should frequently include prayer for the medical professions. If God heals someone directly in answer to prayer, without the need for medical attention, so much the better. But obviously on very many occasions that is not the case. Often we need to pray that the sick person should receive the right medical help, that the doctors may diagnose the sickness correctly, that the right treatment or medication may be given, that they may be effective, and that the patient may be protected from any harmful side-effects.

It has been the experience of many teams praying for healing that in general, where there is authentic prayer for healing, the medical side of things tends to go better. Obviously this does not mean that everyone is physically healed when there is sufficient prayer. There must have been many thousands of Christians praying for David Watson's healing from cancer, and he died. However, in addition to the fruits of peace and spiritual healing – which is always the most important area of healing – prayer for healing can help the physical side of things by relieving pain and distress or producing a remission, even when there is not a complete physical cure.

I remember the case of a married lady in her forties with terminal cancer of the abdomen, whom we visited in a London hospital. The only treatment they could give her at that stage was pain-killers, and they were not being very effective. There was much prayer for healing for her in more than one prayer group. When we prayed for her she felt something like an electric current going through her abdomen, and the pain disappeared on the spot. We were still in the ward when the trolley came round with the pain-killers, and to the surprise of the nurse she declined to take any – and she never needed them again. We wondered for a time whether the cancer was healed, but it was not. She died very peacefully about a month later with no pain at all. The consultant said that the absence of pain was medically speaking totally inexplicable. I have always in my mind linked the healing from pain which she received with the very considerable amount of prayer behind her.

I think of another person, a young mother called R., whose first child was then just a few months old. She developed a very serious cancer condition in the neck area, and medically speaking the outlook was very grim. Members of our healing team prayed with her on many occasions, and there was much prayer for her in her family and in the parish. She received radium and chemotherapy treatment in hospital. The treatment was very surprisingly effective and R. is now, some years later, back at work in the bank and has no cancer. The doctors and medical staff gathered together to give her a very special send-off when she left hospital. One cannot say that R. was healed only through prayer, for obviously the medical treatment was very important. But we do find that medical treatment is more likely to be exceptionally successful when there is much prayer behind it.

Of course there have been the many cases when we have prayed with all our heart for physical healing and for the medical treatment, and things have not gone well physically. There are times when we cannot point to any success at all at the physical level – indeed at any level – in answer to prayer. However, I have never regretted having prayed in these cases. In a way, our job is to pray and results are God's business. In any case we shall never fully know the outcome of our prayers until by the grace of God we get to heaven. Then doubtless we shall have many surprises. Perhaps we shall discover that sometimes when we thought our prayers had failed to help, they were used powerfully. And sometimes when our prayers seemed to have been 'successful', the person would have got better just as well in any case. It may be, for example, that when our prayers failed to relieve pain, they may have been used by God to prevent the pain getting much worse.

Praying for protection against harmful side-effects of medication or other treatment can be very important – as also for the healing of harmful side-effects. In our healing teams we seem to have had especially good results in praying for protection against the unpleasant side-effects of chemotherapy with cancer patients. Indeed, in one particular case the medical staff could not understand why a young lady was feeling no unpleasant side-effects after chemotherapy and why her hair was not falling out – the wig they had prepared for her was never used.

For many people a worrying aspect of much modern medicine is this whole question of the side-effects of medication. It is not all that rare for a medicine to be given to large numbers of people over a considerable number of years – and then for it to be withdrawn or used very sparingly because of the harmful side-effects. I remember trying to help a lady through prayer to come off Valium when medical opinion suddenly changed its attitude to the drug – it was not an easy time for her.

As is well known, quite a high proportion of elderly people who are taken into hospital go there not directly because of an illness but because of trouble caused by medication. Then there is the problem of people being given more and more medicines to counter the side-effects of other medicines. People's eyesight can be adversely affected. I know a person suffering from nervous fears who collapsed into a deep nervous breakdown when he took the first course of medication prescribed by his doctor for his fears. Because of these and other difficulties with medication, an increasing number of people are turning to more natural remedies for healing, such as the use of herbs. I myself would take rose-hip tea rather than an aspirin for a cold.

Against all this one must of course see the many people who

are helped by medication, whose lives have been saved by it. We must also sympathize with doctors in their difficult task of trying to satisfy impatient people who are demanding more medicines to heal their ailments – and this in a very busy surgery where there is little time for each patient. Finally, the rest of us all make mistakes in our work at times, so we cannot expect doctors to be perfect.

However, all this for a Christian surely points in the direction of the desirability of renewing the practice and ministry of praying for healing. More prayer for healing would result in less need to go to doctors, less pressure of numbers in the surgery, less need to take medication or receive other treatment, less trouble with side-effects. I think that if Christians were more faithful to Our Lord's command to heal the sick through prayer, that would be a real blessing not only for the sick themselves but also for the medical services.

Another important dimension of the healing ministry of prayer is the praying done by doctors, nurses and others involved in the medical services. In recent years I have got to know many doctors and nurses who pray very seriously for the healing of their patients and who have the conviction that their prayers make an important difference. I think of two members of our healing prayer team, an orthopaedic surgeon J., and his wife D., who is the head of a therapy department in a large teaching hospital. Some years ago J., who was then working in a London hospital, felt inspired to pray one evening in their hospital prayer group that there would not be the usual casualties from car accidents, fights, muggings, etc., in their catchment area. When he arrived at his fracture clinic thirty-six hours later, he was greeted by the sister who said with amazement that there had been *no* new patients coming in during that period, instead of the usual dozen or so people. He saw this as a sign from God. Since then he and his wife pray daily for their patients, for the staff of their departments and for the people in the catchment areas from which they receive patients. D. finds that her department, with a staff of about thirty people, is running much more successfully since she dedicated it to Jesus; for example, the staff are happier and work better. D. prays with each patient as she treats them. They both have the impression that the medical treatment is in general more effective because of the prayers.

Then there is B., a midwife. She prays daily for her patients before she leaves for work in the morning, and she prays while delivering each baby. She finds that her mothers require stitching considerably less often than is normally the case. She attributes this fact to prayer and not to any special medical skill.

There is also E., a speech therapist, with a powerful gift of healing prayer. She finds that since she came into the Charismatic Renewal and the healing ministry of prayer, her patients in general make both quicker and greater progress.

Another member of our prayer for healing team is B., a consultant surgeon, who normally goes to Mass each morning before work. She prays for all her patients. As she scrubs up before the operation, she says the prayer: 'Spirit of the Living God, fall afresh on me.' As she cuts the skin she does so 'in the name of the Lord'. Nurses tell her that she gets less bleeding with tonsil cases than other surgeons, which she attributes to prayer not skill. Nurses also tell her that 'people say that the patients receive from you more than a medical consultation'. B. tells how in an operation being performed on a man of 45 by her 'boss' in which she was assisting, the man began bleeding profusely and it would not stop. They could not give him a blood transfusion and the situation was very critical. B. began to pray with all her strength and the bleeding stopped, to the surprise of her 'boss' who kept saying: 'I cannot understand why the bleeding stopped.'

Finally, there is J., who is a paediatrician, with a powerful gift of healing prayer. She regularly prays over the new-born babies and sometimes sees remarkable results. Once she woke up in the middle of the night seeing a mental picture of a blue baby, which she knew was a particular baby she was concerned about. So she prayed hard for the baby and in the mental picture the baby turned pink. Next day she discovered that is exactly what happened to the baby in the hospital at the precise time at which she had prayed. And the medical staff with the baby at the time were very surprised at the change and the recovery. J. was also once given by God the diagnosis of a very rare illness from which a baby was suffering. Subsequent investigation proved that she was right, and Europe's top specialist in that particular illness could not understand how J. had managed to diagnose it.

Of course there are many Christian doctors and nurses who pray for their patients and their healing without experiencing the dramatic results which the paediatrician J. quite frequently sees. However, the most important answers to prayer are not necessarily the most dramatic. The vital thing is surely that Christians in the medical services do pray in the way the Holy Spirit leads them for the patients and their healing. The results are God's business!

There is one more subject which needs to be treated at the end of this chapter. There are some Christians who consider that at any rate physical healing is normally a matter for the medical profession, not prayer, but who believe in turning to prayer if the situation is serious and the medical profession cannot help. I think this attitude is mistaken. I am of the opinion that it is normally good to start by praying for healing. If we do this sometimes we shall find that the sickness disappears and that medicine and medical attention are not necessary. However, in certain circumstances it is of course very important not to delay seeking medical help, for example, if someone is bleeding profusely or in real danger of committing suicide. But in these cases, pray on the way to the doctor or the hospital.

Obviously praying for healing must never stand in the way of people receiving the medical help they ought to have. Sometimes the most important thing we have to do is to tell someone to see a doctor. However, the great majority of people who come to us for prayer for healing have already seen doctors or psychiatrists. They come to us because those in the medical profession cannot be of much help. They turn to the only healer who is all powerful, Jesus.

3

Praying for Healing and the Sacraments

The Church itself is the fundamental sacrament: it is also the 'sacrament of universal salvation' (Vatican II, Lumen Gentium no. 48). The Church as the Body of Christ is called to continue Christ's healing mission. Everything in the Church should in one way or another participate in this work of salvation, this work of healing. Canon law, curial offices, church bazaars, church buildings and all that happens within them should contribute in one way or another to the Church's work of salvation, its ministry of healing – and if anything is not contributing, then there is something wrong with it.

The traditional seven sacraments of the Church participate in a special way in the healing ministry of the Church. They are all of them channels through which flow the healing love of Jesus. Baptism signifies the passage from darkness into light, the entry into God's Kingdom, the healing of original sin. Confirmation by strengthening and empowering us helps to heal our weakness. Marriage can be and should be for the spouses a deeply healing experience, and their home should be a place where all who enter receive healing of one kind or another. The Sacrament of Orders can and should be not only a healing experience for the priest himself, but also help him to be a source of healing love for others in every aspect of his priestly ministry. The healing qualities of the remaining sacraments I will now treat at greater length.

The Sacrament of Reconciliation

The Sacrament of Penance or Reconciliation is referred to in the official introduction to the rite (no. 7) as 'this sacrament of healing'. It is a channel for the healing of sin, for the receiving of God's forgiveness, for reconciliation with God and our neighbours.

It is a pity that in recent years many Catholics have more or less turned their back on this sacrament, thus depriving themselves of an important source of healing. We are all sinners, and we all need to repent, to turn away from sin towards God and the things of God. Indeed, we should repent daily – and of course repentance should not be confined to the sacrament of penance. However, the sacrament can help to focus and deepen our repentance, especially if we periodically – and not too infrequently – confess our sins to a priest and receive absolution. Confession has its own special sacramental grace, and who has not felt spiritually lighter and less burdened as they walk away after receiving absolution?

However, confession is not magic. We do not automatically receive the grace of the sacrament regardless of our dispositions. If we are to receive the full benefit of this sacrament, we need to prepare ourselves seriously, to be truly sorry for our sins, to want really to avoid sin in the future, and to call on the mercy of the Lord with all our mind and heart.

In his excellent small book, *The Power in Penance* (Ave Maria Press, 1972), Father Michael Scanlon TOR suggests that the priest should often pray for healing and strengthening after giving absolution. I have found as a priest that people in general welcome a prayer for healing and strengthening after receiving absolution. Such prayer will normally concentrate on spiritual and emotional healing, but it can also include physical healing. Sick people in hospital have often warmly welcomed the offer to pray for the healing of their physical sickness after confession – and physical improvement has sometimes followed. It seems that not so infrequently God chooses to heal people physically after they have confessed their sins.

One further point about confession: the sharing with another human being of our weaknesses, trials, temptations and sins can be a very healing experience. It can be a great relief to free the bottled up guilt and get it off one's chest. For me personally it is a source of peace that there is no conscious area of my past, however shameful or dark or humiliating, that I have not shared with a confessor. And the humbling of ourselves which such sharing requires is part of the healing process. Furthermore, a wise confessor is able, with the help of the Holy Spirit, to discern our needs and give wise advice. This wise counselling is normally a necessary part of the process of inner healing which we all need.

All this emphasizes the need for the confessor and the penitent to pray seriously to the Holy Spirit for light, love and healing before the confession. We should expect the Holy Spirit to come with power when this sacrament is celebrated – even though we may not always feel the power. We shall see more of this power and healing as we pray more truly: 'Come, Holy Spirit.'

The sacrament of the anointing of the sick

> And they cast out many demons, and anointed with oil many that were sick and healed them. (Mark 6:13)

> Is any among you sick? Let him call for the elders of the church, and let them pray over him, anointing him with oil in the name of the Lord; and the prayer of faith will save the sick man, and the Lord will raise him up; and if he has committed sins, he will be forgiven. Therefore confess your sins to one another, and pray for one another, that you may be healed. (James 5:14–16)

Pope Paul VI in the Apostolic Constitution introducing the official rite for the Sacrament of the Anointing of the Sick links this sacrament with the above passages in the New Testament, especially with the passage from James. Given these clear refer-

ences in the New Testament to the anointing with oil for healing, it is not surprising that there have always been Christians
down the centuries who continued to anoint the sick with oil
as they prayed for healing. What is surprising however is that
greater use has not been made of this New Testament practice.
There have been sections of the Protestant world which ceased
anointing the sick with oil for healing. And for centuries Catholics of the Latin Rite only gave this anointing to the dying,
thus severely limiting the use made of this sacrament. Let us
thank God that in our own times the anointing of the sick with
oil for healing is becoming more widespread again, both among
Protestants and Catholics.

It is important to realize that the administration and use
made of this sacrament has varied very considerably during the
history of the Catholic Church – and doubtless there will be
further changes. Until the beginning of the ninth century the
stress seems to have been on healing, especially physical healing. The bishop or priest blessed the oil, which the faithful
often took home with them, anointing themselves or each other
as the need arose. The main purpose of the sacrament was seen
as the healing of the sick. From the beginning of the ninth
century there was a move towards limiting the task of anointing
to the clergy, and the sacrament was increasingly seen as a
spiritual help for the dying, which included the forgiveness of
sins. So a sacrament for the healing of the sick became mainly
the last anointing of the dying, Extreme Unction.

The Second Vatican Council (1962–5) made very important
changes in the use of this sacrament, taking more into account
the healing thrust of the New Testament texts and of the tradition of the first eight centuries. So the Sacrament of Extreme
Unction had its name changed to the Sacrament of the Anointing of the Sick.

The official General Introduction of the Rites of Anointing
and Viaticum (1972) gives us encouragement in the ministry of
praying for healing. 'Part of the plan laid out by God's providence is that we should fight strenuously against all sickness

and carefully seek the blessings of good health, so that we may fulfill our role in human society and in the Church' (no. 3).

The following quotations from the same source will help people to understand the official teaching and instruction of the Catholic Church on this sacrament after Vatican II:

A return to physical health may follow the reception of this sacrament if it will be beneficial to the sick person's salvation. If necessary, the sacrament also provides the sick person with the forgiveness of sins and the completion of Christian penance.   (No. 6)

Great care and concern should be taken to see that those of the faithful whose health is seriously impaired by sickness or old age receive this sacrament.   (No. 8)

The sacrament may be repeated if the sick person recovers after being anointed and then again falls ill or if during the same illness the person's condition becomes more serious.
(No. 9)

A sick person may be anointed before surgery whenever a serious illness is the reason for the surgery.   (No. 10)

Elderly people may be anointed if they have become notably weakened even though no serious illness is present.
(No. 11)

In public and private catechesis, the faithful should be educated to ask for the sacrament of anointing and, as soon as the right time comes, to receive it with full faith and they should not follow the wrongful practice of delaying the reception of the sacrament. All who care for the sick should be taught the meaning and purpose of the sacrament. (No. 13)

Some types of mental sickness are now classified as serious. Those who are judged to have a serious mental illness and who would be strengthened by the sacrament may be anointed (see no. 5). The anointing may be repeated in accordance with the conditions for other kinds of serious illness. (See no. 9.)   (No. 53)

The healing intention of this sacrament is clearly seen in the very beautiful prayer which the priest uses for the blessing of the oil when it has not been already blessed by the bishop:

God of all consolation,
you chose and sent your Son to heal the world.
Graciously listen to our prayer of faith:
send the power of your Holy Spirit, the Consoler,
into this precious oil, this soothing ointment,
this rich gift, this fruit of the earth.

Bless this oil + and sanctify it for our use.
Make this oil a remedy for all who are anointed with it;
heal them in body, in soul, and in spirit,
and deliver them from every affliction.

We ask this through our Lord Jesus Christ, your Son,
who lives and reigns with you and the Holy Spirit,
one God, for ever and ever.

Mistranslation

In his excellent article on this sacrament in the Faith Alive series in the *Universe* (no. 38, 1987), Father Christopher O'Donnell o CARM points out that a very unfortunate mistranslation in the English text of the Code of Canon Law – 'the editors have since admitted this serious mistake' – has led some priests to be too restrictive in the administration of this sacrament. The latin word 'periculum' (danger) has been translated 'danger of death'. But there are of course other dangers – dangers of going blind, deaf, paralyzed, depressed, senile, etc. So some priests are wanting only to administer this sacrament when there is danger of death. It could be a very helpful thing to refer these priests to Father O'Donnell's article and point out the mistranslation.

May I make a plea for a more generous use of this sacrament? May I especially ask some of the Catholic clergy to reconsider their attitudes and practice, to break away from the pre-Vatican

II mentality? I am often deeply saddened – and indeed I can feel angry – when I come across practising Catholics who could and should have received this sacrament but have not done so because the clergy have refrained from giving it. I think, for example, of numerous practising Catholics suffering seriously from depression for years to whom the clergy have failed to suggest that they could be anointed. Only yesterday a devout Catholic man told me of his struggle over years to recover from the serious side-effects of the chemotherapy given him for cancer. He praised the kindness of the Catholic chaplain in the hospital. The chaplain however had never suggested that he could be anointed. If we believe in the power of prayer, if we take seriously the prayers for healing in the rite of anointing, if we believe in the power of the sacraments, then surely we must realize that this man's struggle – and the struggle of many others – to regain his health could well have been greatly helped by the receiving of the Sacrament of the Anointing of the Sick. Jesus in his infinite love and wisdom has given us this wonderful healing sacrament for helping and healing sick people. And we frequently leave the seriously sick struggling and suffering with an illness without giving them the help of this sacrament. May Jesus forgive us!

The problem however is not only one of the pre-Vatican II approach of some of the clergy (and the laity) and the mistranslation into English of canon law. There is also the factor of the shortage of clergy, which is sometimes very acute. If a priest has far too much to do, he inevitably cannot do his job properly – and many overburdened priests are managing much better than I would do in their circumstances! The excellent article on the anointing of the sick in the *New Dictionary of Theology* (Gill and Macmillan, Dublin, 1987) makes the point clearly: 'A conflict results from the Vatican Council's encouragement to receive the sacrament yet an insufficient number of priestly ministers to make it available.' This article envisages the possibility that lay people could be allowed to administer this sacrament, a point also made by two Jesuit priests: 'Just as lay people are once again becoming ministers of the Eucharist, they may also again become ministers of the Sacrament of the Sick' (page 19, *To Heal as Jesus Healed* by Barbara Leahy Schlemon, Dennis Linn SJ and Matthew Linn SJ, Ave Maria Press, 1978). It is not difficult to see that if certain doctors, nurses and parish workers were able to administer this sacrament, then many people who at present die or suffer without receiving it would be able to be anointed. For instance, dying people brought into a hospital could be immediately anointed by a nurse, when a priest could not get there in time. There is also the fact that people are understandably reluctant to make calls on the time and energy of over-stretched clergy, when they would not hesitate to call in an authorized lay person. This would perhaps be especially true when it is a question of repeating the anointing, which sometimes is both highly desirable and entirely permissible. Just as the introduction of lay ministers of the Eucharist has been a great blessing in both allowing sick people to receive communion more often and in relieving the overburdened clergy of unnecessary work, so I think that the return to lay administration of this sacrament would be a similar blessing all round.

A practice which is being found very fruitful in some parishes is that of regularly holding services in which the sick of the parish receive the Sacrament of the Anointing of the Sick together – rather like the services of anointing in Lourdes. These services can be beautiful occasions on which the parish as a whole prays for its sick members and expresses its loving concern for them. The service can be followed by refreshments and the giving of presents.

Needless to say the wider use of this sacrament should not be carried to excess. Obviously the sacrament should not be trivialized or administered indiscriminately. However it is important not to be over-scrupulous. As a priest I would prefer to come before the judgment seat of God having given this sacrament too easily rather than having been too restrictive. After all, if it is by mistake given too easily, no great harm is done. But it is surely no small thing to deprive a genuinely needy person of the help this sacrament can give. In the USA the bishops have officially included such things as 'spiritual aridity' as something for which a person can be anointed. Let us not be too hesitant on this side of the Atlantic!

The Holy Eucharist

The celebration of the Holy Eucharist is in the first place for the purpose of giving thanks and glory to God. Asking for things for creatures is secondary to the theme of praise. However the celebration of the Holy Eucharist is also the most powerful form of intercession. And prayer for healing in one form or another is an important theme in every Mass.

All Christians believe in praying for spiritual healing, which is of course the most important area of healing. However many Christians, including quite a few Catholics, say that they do not believe in praying for physical healing. There are even Catholic priests who celebrate Mass daily, with all the texts in the Mass which pray for healing, and yet apparently do not believe in praying for physical healing! There is the contrast between the liturgy, which is rich in prayers for healing, and the intellectual ideas of many Catholics, who are either very sceptical about praying for physical healing or simply do not believe in it.

Let us now turn to a few healing texts in the liturgy of the Mass, some of which explicitly include physical healing.

In one of the personal liturgical prayers of the priest before communion, I frequently say: 'Lord Jesus Christ, with faith in your love and mercy I eat your body and drink your blood. Let it not bring me condemnation, but health in mind and body.'

The opening prayer of the Mass of Our Lady, which I and many other priests celebrate on most Saturdays, commences: 'Lord God, give to your people the joy of continual health in mind and body.'

As Father Jim McManus CSSR points out in his excellent book, *The Healing Power of the Sacraments* (Ave Maria Press, 1984), quite a few of the post-communion prayers ask for healing, for example, the one from the Monday of the First Week in Lent: 'Lord, through this sacrament may we rejoice in your healing power and experience your love in mind and body.'

The most important healing text in the Mass, however, is surely the prayer we all say immediately before communion: 'Lord, I am not worthy to receive you, but only say the word and I shall be healed.' (The earlier translation read: 'But only say the word and my soul shall be healed.' The Church changed the 'my soul' to 'I' precisely to include physical healing.)

There are other prayers in the Mass which refer directly to health and healing. 'You were sent to heal the contrite: Lord, have mercy' (from the Penitential Rite). One of the blessings for Holy Water reads: 'Lord God Almighty, creator of life, of body and soul, we ask you to bless this water: as we use it in faith forgive our sins and save us from all illness and the power of evil.'

However, there are other prayers in the Mass which are essentially healing prayers, which include healing without using the words 'healing' and 'health'. For example, the words from the consecration: 'It will be shed for you and for all men so that sins may be forgiven'; the prayers for the repose of the departed; 'Deliver us, Lord, from every evil, and grant us peace in our day'; 'The peace of the Lord be with you always'; 'May all of us who share in the body and blood of Christ be brought together in unity by the Holy Spirit' (Eucharistic Prayer 2).

The Mass is in the first place a great prayer of praise, of giving glory and adoration to God. It is also however a great prayer for healing – healing at every level, the individual and the community, the Church and the world, the levels of the spirit, the mind and the body. So let us preach and teach more about this healing dimension of the Mass; let us as we participate in the Mass be more aware of this healing dimension; let us at Mass implore Jesus to fill us and others with his healing love. Especially when we go to communion let us ask Jesus to fill us with his healing love, for in communion we receive the same Jesus who nearly two thousand years ago went about Israel healing the sick, and his healing touch has lost none of its power. 'Lord, I am not worthy to receive you, but only say the word and I shall be healed.' Every communion can and should surely be a healing, strengthening occasion. I think it can be good in general when we receive communion to pray for the healing, strengthening and protecting of spirit, mind and body. Certainly the spiritual healing is the most important area – but why leave out the mind and the body? Is Jesus now no longer interested in healing minds and bodies? Is he no longer capable of healing them? Where is our faith in his love and power?

Notice that I also suggested praying for strengthening and protecting. Modern medicine is more and more interested in the prevention of sickness. Should not our prayers in connection with healing include the dimensions of strengthening and protecting? Why wait until something has gone wrong before we call upon the healing power of Jesus?

Sister Briege McKenna osc, in her remarkable book, *Miracles Do Happen* (Veritas Publications, 1987), explains how, as she goes round the world, her healing ministry is increasingly centred on the healing power of Jesus in the Holy Eucharist. She was amazed when at a Mass attended by many poor people in Latin America, she saw two children receive miraculous physical healings, and this gave her a new awareness of the healing power of Jesus in the Holy Eucharist. She tells of a woman who had a large stomach cancer which caused great swelling. Sister Briege said to the woman:

Go to meet Jesus in the Eucharist. While I can't tell anyone they will be healed the way they want because I'm not God, Jesus will supply you with the strength to face whatever is on your road of life. If he is going to bring you through the door of death, he will give you the grace to go through that door without this awful fear. And if you are to live, he will give you the grace to live.

When the woman went to communion she prayed: 'I know you are really here. Today when you come into me, take away this fear. Heal me if you want, but please do something for me.'

The woman was in fact healed of the cancer. 'I had no sooner put the Host on my tongue and swallowed it than I felt as though something was burning my throat and down into my stomach. I looked down at my stomach and the growth was gone' (page 67).

Sister Briege also tells of how people are sometimes healed when they are blessed with the Holy Eucharist. A young Mormon girl in Hawaii was present at a healing service, and when the crowd was blessed with the Holy Eucharist her painful and deformed hands were healed (page 113).

For every case of a remarkable physical miracle such as the two recounted above, there are surely thousands of people who regularly look to the Lord in the Holy Eucharist to heal, strengthen and sustain them at every level – and the Lord answers their prayers in ways which go well beyond what was to be expected at the purely human level. I think of a good friend of mine who is the co-ordinator of a large prayer group and whose lungs have been seriously sick for years. What greatly surprises the doctors is that someone with her lungs can live the very active and fruitful life she does. The healing and strengthening power of Jesus in the Eucharist is surely in her case a large part of the explanation.

Sacramentals

At the end of this chapter on the sacraments it seems appropriate to write briefly on sacramentals, especially one of them. It is in the Catholic tradition to use sacramentals such as holy water, holy medals, holy statues, holy pictures, icons, beads, scapulars, blessed salt and blessed oil. It can be good to make use of sacramentals for healing and protection insofar as they are found helpful. However, it is important to remember that it is Jesus who heals and protects, not the holy water, the medals, or other sacramentals. It is also important to avoid any suggestion of magic or superstition: people are healed because Jesus wants to heal them, not because they possess a particular statue or a holy medal.

There is one sacramental which I want particularly to mention, since many Catholics are finding it helpful in connection with healing. There is in the Roman Ritual a blessing for olive oil (or other vegetable oil) which lay people can use for healing or other suitable purposes. The oil has to be blessed by a priest, but lay people can apply it to themselves or others. It can be good to anoint the sick part of the body with this oil as far as that is possible. And the anointing can be repeated as often as seems appropriate, for example, daily. I know of one case in which a man was healed of terminal cancer after being extensively anointed with this blessed oil. I know of another case in which an elderly woman regularly received relief from pain after the anointing. Yesterday a man told me that when he cannot sleep, he anoints himself with oil and sleep invariably follows quickly. Indeed, not infrequently we receive reports of good things happening after people have been anointed with this oil.

This blessed oil is sometimes referred to as the Oil of Gladness, to distinguish it from that used in the Sacrament of the Anointing of the Sick. Members of healing teams and others anointing people with this oil should, when necessary, clearly explain that it is not the Sacrament of the Sick.

Needless to say, the use of the blessed oil, like everything else in the healing ministry of prayer, is subject to any diocesan or other regulations which may have been made by the competent authority in the Church.

Since very few priests possess a copy of the complete Roman Ritual, it will be useful to give here the text of this ancient blessing of oil:

BLESSING OF OIL, FOR USE BY LAITY

Our help is in the name of the Lord,
R. Who made heaven and earth.

(Exorcism)

God's creature, oil,
I cast out the demon from you by God the Father Almighty,

who made heaven and earth and sea and all that they contain.
Let the adversary's power, the devil's legions,
and all Satan's attacks and machinations
be dispelled and driven afar
from this creature oil.

Let it bring health in body and mind to all who use it,
in the name of God + the Father Almighty,
and our Lord Jesus Christ + his Son,
and the Holy Spirit + the Advocate,
as well as in the love of the same Jesus Christ our Lord,
who is coming to judge both the living and the dead
and the world by fire.

R. Amen.

Lord, heed my prayer,
R. And let my cry be heard by you.
The Lord be with you,
R. And also with you.

Let us pray.

Lord God Almighty,
before whom the hosts of angels stand in awe
and whose heavenly service we acknowledge,
may it please you to regard favourably and bless and hallow
this creature oil,
which by your power has been pressed from the juice of olives.
You have ordained it for anointing the sick, so that,
when they are made well,
they may give thanks to you,
the living and true God.
Grant we pray,
that those who use this oil,
which we are blessing + in your name,
may be delivered from all suffering,
all infirmity,
and all wiles of the enemy.

Let it be a means of averting any kind of adversity from man, made in your image and redeemed by the precious blood of your Son, so that he may never again suffer the sting of the ancient serpent, through Christ our Lord.

R. Amen.

(The oil is sprinkled with holy water)*

*The Roman Ritual, translated by Philip Weller (Milwaukee, Bruce, 1964, page 573).

4

Does God Always Want to Heal? Those Who Are Not Healed

As we saw in Chapter 1, Jesus commanded his disciples to heal the sick in his name: 'And he called the twelve together and gave them power and authority over all demons and to cure diseases, and he sent them out to preach the Kingdom of God and to heal. . . . And they departed and went through the villages preaching the gospel and healing everywhere' (Luke 9:1ff). Jesus also promised that: 'these signs will accompany those who believe: in my name they will cast out demons; . . . they will lay their hands on the sick, and they will recover' (Mark 16:17).

Does this mean that Jesus wants to heal every sickness in this life? Some Christians would reply 'yes' to that question. They would say that: 'by his cross you are saved and by his stripes you are healed' (cf. Isaiah 53:5; 1 Peter 2:24). We know that God wants to save everyone. They would say that in the same way God wants to heal every sickness in this life. Both are for them the fruit of the Atonement. It must be said that some of the Christians who take this line are very successful in their healing ministry, that remarkable healings take place in their healing services. They preach with great faith and fervour the message that Jesus wants to heal all sickness, and quite a few people are healed, including sometimes remarkable physical healings. This approach has the advantage of being single-minded in its aim – to heal every sickness in everyone.

However, the 'Jesus-always-wants-to-heal-all-sickness' approach has its disadvantages. What happens to the people who are not healed? If someone is told that Jesus certainly wants to heal his or her terminal cancer or blindness, and the cancer or the blindness is not healed, how does the sick person feel? Surely they will often either feel guilty: 'Jesus wants to heal me. I am not healed. It must be due to my lack of faith or sinfulness'; or they will blame those who prayed for their healing: 'they did not pray enough, or their ministry is not powerful enough'; or they will lose faith in Jesus: 'I can no longer believe in this Jesus who has not healed me'; or they will simply turn their back on all praying for healing of any kind. I can remember a case in which an Anglican vicar complained bitterly that the faith of a dying parishioner which he had been carefully nurturing was shattered after some charismatic Christians came and prayed over her for healing, giving the impression that Jesus wanted to heal her physically. She was not healed physically and went through a total crisis of faith.

Experiences of this kind may help to explain why some Christians, especially some of the clergy, can be put off all praying for healing. Perhaps they have experienced cases in which people appear to have been harmed or really have been harmed rather than helped by prayer for healing. If it is claimed that Jesus certainly wants to heal every sickness in this life, then people who are not healed can come away from a healing service confused, discouraged and with weakened faith.

The advocates of the 'Jesus-always-wants-to-heal-every-sickness' approach also have to face honestly the fact that even with the most powerful healing ministries the great majority of terminally ill people die, the great majority of blind people remain blind, the great majority of people with schizophrenia continue to have schizophrenia. Indeed we rightly consider it very wonderful when a small minority of them are miraculously healed. So what are we to think of the many people who are not healed at that level? If Jesus wants to heal every sickness in this life, then even the most powerful healing ministries are dismal failures. For every person at a Kathryn Kuhlman healing service who got up from their wheelchair and walked, there must have been hundreds who could not do so. The 'Jesus-always-wants-to-heal-every-sickness' approach simply does not seem to stand up to the test of what really happens even in the most fervent Christian communities. And this is especially true if we consider those who are seriously handicapped physically or mentally from birth, very few of whom are miraculously healed.

There is a further problem with this approach. If one concentrates on praying for the healing of the terminal cancer, for example, then one surely cannot prepare the sick person spiritually for death in an adequate manner. Surely the time comes when the right thing to pray for is a peaceful and blessed death, not the miraculous healing of cancer. I have frequently started by praying for a physical healing miracle with a seriously sick person, and later as their health declined have changed the general orientation to praying for a blessed death. But if Jesus always wants to heal sickness in this life, then obviously one should go on praying for the physical miracle to the very end, which may not be helpful to the dying person. (Everyone admits of course that there comes a time for a person in ripe old age to pass peacefully into eternity with Jesus. The problem we are dealing with here is that of people who have not reached that stage in their lives.)

Is there not another possibility somewhere between the 'Jesus-always-wants-to-heal' approach outlined above and the current practice of most Christian congregations of not praying for physical healing, or of praying for it in a very half-hearted way? Yes, there is. It is the approach which has normally been adopted in the Catholic Charismatic Renewal – and not only there – and which Francis MacNutt describes in his important books: *Healing* (1974) and *The Power to Heal* (1977), both published by the Ave Maria Press in the USA.

In this approach Christians are encouraged to pray seriously for healing, including normally physical healing, in obedience to the instructions of Jesus. But it is recognized that Jesus may not want to heal every physical and mental sickness in this life. Jesus may have a purpose of redemptive suffering in an illness for a time or more than a time. In such cases not only will the sickness not be healed in answer to prayer, but the person receiving prayer should be willing to accept the sickness and the suffering it involves.

Catholics sometimes feel in a dilemma over the question of sickness and prayer. Should they adopt the line that Jesus always wants to heal and that we must simply pray with ever greater faith and perseverance for healing? Or should they see sickness as a suffering to be accepted and offered up in prayer for redemptive purposes, remembering the words of St Paul: 'Now I rejoice in my sufferings for your sake, and in my flesh I complete what is lacking in Christ's afflictions for the sake of his body, that is, the church' (Colossians 1:24)? I think that the answer to the apparent dilemma is that we need to use and harmonize the two approaches, because neither by itself is right for every situation. We should normally start by praying for the healing of spirit, mind and body. Jesus always wants to heal us more spiritually, so we know that when we pray for healing he always wants us to receive some healing, at least at the spiritual level. However, I think Jesus frequently also wants us to receive healing at the levels of the mind and the body. So we should normally also pray for mental and physical healing with faith and perseverance, but realizing that Jesus may not want to answer our prayer in the way we first hoped.

I have over the years prayed for thousands of people for physical healing who apparently received no physical healing. I have prayed for hundreds of people who experienced some physical improvement – even though often it was only small. I have never regretted praying for physical healing for those who apparently received no physical healing. I always also prayed for their spiritual and emotional/mental healing. Often they received great peace even when there was no physical improvement. If I had not been willing normally to pray for physical healing, then those who in fact did receive some physical healing would not have done so. I have never reproached myself about praying for physical healing which did not happen. I would however have felt bad about not having tried, because then I would wonder whether if I had, perhaps that person would have received some physical healing, some relief from pain.

Some people in the healing ministry are more gifted than I am in listening to God, and God will show them more often whether he wants to heal someone physically or not. So their prayer for the sick will be led more directly by 'words' from above. People who are more gifted in this field should thank God for their gifts and use them. However, no one receives a 'word' for every case; and these 'words' are at any rate not infallible. Moreover, one cannot easily say to someone who asks you to pray for the healing of cancer in their child: 'No, I will not pray for the healing of the cancer.' However, if God seems to be showing us something, then that can influence the balance and general direction of our prayer.

For me the truth that our sufferings, including suffering from illness can through God's grace be redemptive is a very important part of the good news of the Christian gospel. Suffering is not something to speak lightly about, especially when it is severe. The idea of severe suffering which is meaningless and fruitless is a very terrible one. The New Testament tells us that by the grace of God our sufferings, united with the sufferings of Jesus, can be redemptive, can be very fruitful for ourselves and others, can be very meaningful. (See Colossians 1:24 quoted above. See also Hebrews 12:3–11; James 1:2–4 and 12; 1 Peter 1:6–7 and 4:12–13.) So it can be important to tell a person that their sufferings can be meaningful and redemptive, while at the same time we pray for healing of the sickness and the pain. This knowledge can help them to bear the suffering and can bring them peace. I think of a woman suffering much from a rare arthritic condition over whom several of us have prayed for healing. She continues to suffer much physical pain, especially when she reduces the steroids and other drugs. If we had not prayed perhaps she would have suffered still more from the illness and from the side-effects of the drugs. We must certainly go on praying for the healing of the sickness and pain. But it has been important to let her know that her sufferings can be, are being, fruitful redemptively, and to pray that God will give her the strength to bear them.

In the healing ministry of our prayer group in Cockfosters we have seen cancer patients healed physically in answer to prayer, and we have seen people dying from cancer receive great courage and peace, great spiritual healing. I think of John – not his real name – a medical doctor in his thirties, with a young family, who was lying paralyzed in his bed at home with cancer in his back, and his wife had been told that he was expected to die within three months. Another medical doctor asked a woman in our healing team if she would go and pray with John for healing. So she and a few others visited John and prayed over him on numerous occasions – I myself was little involved in this ministry. John is now back at work as a doctor in a hospital, and he has been told by the specialists that he is free from cancer – and you should see the wonderful smile on his face as he tells you about his healing.

Alongside John I think of James – not his real name. James was also in his thirties, the father of young children, and he also had terminal cancer. Our healing team also prayed over James for healing on numerous occasions. James came back to the sacraments, received wonderful spiritual healing, was given great peace and strength – and went to live with Jesus in heaven.

One thing, I think, especially needs to be said about John and James. We cannot say that the healing John received from Jesus was more important than the healing James received from him. God alone knows the answer to that question. I think that Jesus healed John in the way he wanted to, and that he also healed James in the way he wanted to. As Kathryn Kuhlman used to say, it is part of the mystery of God's loving providence why one person is physically healed and another is not. As she pointed out, sometimes a person with little or no faith is physically healed, while a Christian with great faith is not. We simply have to accept the mystery of God's loving providence for each individual.

I think that many people with terminal illnesses are not

healed in answer to prayer simply because the right time has come for that person to go to Jesus in heaven, because he or she has finished the work which God gave them to do on earth. 'Thy eyes beheld my unformed substance; in thy book were written, every one of them, the days that were formed for me, when as yet there was none of them' (Psalm 139(138):16). This is perhaps the place to remember that death for the Christian is the passage to the fuller life with Jesus, that all physical healing is in one sense temporary, and that none of us will be perfectly healed all round until we are with Jesus in heaven.

Life in heaven is very much better than life on earth. When we pray for the healing of terminal illnesses we do so in so far as the person has not finished the work God may want him or her to do on earth. We are not trying to keep people out of heaven for a day longer than God wants. St Paul, writing to the Philippians from prison, when it was uncertain whether he would be put to death or not, put things in the right perspective.

> For me to live is Christ, and to die is gain. If it is to be life in the flesh, that means fruitful labour for me. Yet which I shall choose I cannot tell. I am hard pressed between the two. My desire is to depart and be with Christ, for that is far better. But to remain in the flesh is more necessary on your account. Convinced of this, I know that I shall remain and continue with you all, for your progress and joy in the faith. (Philippians 1:21–5)

Some writers have objected that the redemptive suffering alluded to in the New Testament is not that caused by sickness, but the sufferings of persecution which come from being a Christian. So they conclude that the sufferings caused by illness are not to be seen as redemptive, as part of the cross Jesus asks us to take up. I would disagree with this view. I think the sufferings of St Paul's illness in Galatians (4:13) and Timothy's 'frequent ailments' (1 Timothy 5:23) were redemptive and contributed to their spiritual growth. (Often we find today that people grow spiritually during the course of a serious illness.) I regard it as most important not to deprive people who have not been healed physically by prayer of the consolation of knowing that the sufferings caused by their illness can be, indeed are being, redemptive – even though we may rightly continue to pray for physical healing and the relief of suffering.

A last point: when it comes to praying for healing for people with terminal cancer and similar diseases, those of us in the healing ministry need to admit that there are always far more James than Johns, that outstanding physical healing miracles are the exception rather than the rule everywhere. Let us thank God for the outstanding miracles. Let us regret that they are absent in so many Christian congregations. I am sure that Jesus wants to work far more physical healing miracles in our churches. Let us encourage many more Christians to pray for physical healing. Let us hope and indeed expect to see far more physical healing miracles. Let us pray and fast for them. But let us not claim that a physical healing miracle should be normal in every case of serious physical sickness, that God wants to do physical healing miracles for everyone.

5

Praying For Healing • I

Praying for healing is not a matter of mastering a technique, of learning precise formulas, of following a set of rules. It is Jesus who heals people not us, and he heals people when and how he wills. So all we can do is to beg him in his infinite mercy to bless people with his healing touch of love. Basically what is required of us is that we try to pray authentically, which means that we seek to pray with faith, hope, love and humility.

Over the years I have noticed with interest how God has led various people who are gifted in the healing ministry to pray in different styles. Ian Andrews, Monsignor Michael Buckley, John Wimber, Trevor Dearing and the Jesuit Linn brothers, all have their own style of praying. The Holy Spirit leads no two people to pray for healing in exactly the same way. The important thing is that we pray as the Holy Spirit guides us.

Having said that, we can recognize that there are certain general rules which experience shows are normally helpful or indeed necessary when praying for healing. So in this chapter I shall attempt to formulate some of these in the form of general guide-lines.

Prayer preparation and support

Clearly it is highly desirable to prepare ourselves when possible through prayer (and perhaps fasting) before going to pray with a sick person or participate in the ministry in a healing service. What happens or does not happen when we pray with a sick person can be as dependent or even more dependent on the prayers we say beforehand, as on the prayers we say at the time. Sometimes, of course, we are asked to pray with someone without warning, so we cannot consciously pray for that particular person beforehand. But people specially involved in the healing ministry of prayer will normally pray daily for their healing ministry in general, so that when they are suddenly called upon to pray with someone unexpectedly their ministry has already been commended to the Lord.

One very remarkable and unusual example of prayer preparation for the healing ministry was the late J. Cameron Peddie, who helped greatly to pioneer the healing ministry of prayer in the Presbyterian Church of Scotland. Before he started praying for healing with people, he prayed for one hour a day for five years to prepare himself for this ministry. No wonder miracles started to happen when he began to lay hands on the sick!

However, it is not only good that we ourselves pray for the healing of sick persons before we visit or are visited by them. Perhaps far more important is often asking other people to pray (and perhaps fast) for them and their healing. Frequently before I am going to pray with a sick person I telephone around to several people asking them to pray, or I ask all the members present at a prayer group to pray. Over and over again I have found that when more people are supporting with prayer, more good things seem to happen in the healing ministry.

So a key element in all healing ministry is to try to get sufficient prayer backing. The intercessors behind the scenes may sometimes do far more for healing than those who lay hands on the sick. One can but commend the example of the London Healing Mission which has a group of over 700 registered intercessors who pray daily for their healing ministry and who each receive every month a list of five names to pray for especially. There are also the lists of sick people to be prayed for in many parishes, which encourage praying for healing.

The importance of praise

A weakness of much healing ministry is the lack of praise and thanksgiving. In 1 Peter 2:9 we read that we are 'a people set apart to sing the praises of God'; and the psalmist says: 'I will bless the Lord at all times; his praise shall continually be in my mouth' (Psalm 34 (33):1). Sometimes when there is sufficient praise, people get healed in spirit, mind or body without even asking for healing. At other times a person's sickness only begins to improve when the healing team's or congregation's praise increases – I remember seeing a lady's foot visibly improving as members of our healing team praying with her gave themselves to inspired and lengthy praise. (Her foot began shaking strongly – shaking is frequently a sign of healing – and afterwards she found that she had greater mobility in the foot.)

Some people at a healing service or session mistakenly think that the period of praise at the beginning is a kind of hors-d'oeuvre before getting down to the really serious business of praying for healing. This view is profoundly mistaken. Nothing is more important than praise and thanksgiving when we are praying for healing. Praise is the only right setting in which to undertake this ministry. Our intercessions should be shot through with praise and thanksgiving. We should not praise God in order that people may be healed. We should praise him because that is the right thing to do in any case, praise him whether people are healed in body or not. However, as our praises ascend his blessings descend, and they will include healing in one form or another. The emphasis should be on praising and thanking God and Jesus with all our hearts, minds and souls. Praising God is a fulfilling of the first commandment.

Praying for protection

It is also good not only to praise but also to pray for protection at the beginning of a healing service or session. When we are praying for healing we may find ourselves involved in spiritual warfare. In a healing service or session there is not only the possibility of good things happening, there is also the possibility that things may go wrong, although this happens only very rarely in my experience. So it is important to pray for protection for everyone involved: those praying for healing, those being prayed with and everyone else present.

I often use the following prayer: 'Jesus, through your Precious Blood, protect us from all harm, evil and attacks of the devil now, at times of special difficulty or danger, and for evermore. Amen.' I also make the sign of the cross, which can be a powerful form of protection. I also sometimes use holy water.

Although it is wise and right to pray for protection at the beginning of a healing service or session, this prayer should not be over-emphasized or take too long.

Praying for healing of spirit, mind and body

When we pray with people for healing we should pray for the healing of spirit, mind and body, for they are closely inter-related. Whatever affects one of these parts of our being has an influence of one kind or another on the other two. The holistic approach is spreading increasingly in modern medicine, where the tendency is to look more at the whole person and not just at the separate parts.

This approach means that we do not like praying only for the health of the body. I normally start by praying for spiritual and mental or emotional healing before I pray for the well-being of the body. This seems to be the right way round, not only because spiritual healing is the most important area of healing, but also because spiritual and mental or emotional sickness quite often cause physical sickness – and quite often the physical healing will not take place until people have been healed at the other levels.

Spiritual healing

Sin is spiritual sickness. And since we are all sinners, we all need further spiritual healing. Repentance is the door which opens the way to receive God's forgiveness and spiritual healing. Thus in the healing ministry we often need to lead people in the way of repentance. On many occasions I have helped people to make an act of repentance and not infrequently this has ended with the Sacrament of Reconciliation. People often look on repentance as something negative, gloomy, unpleasant. We need to show people that repentance is on the contrary cleansing, healing, liberating, life giving, joyful!

After repenting we should pray for the virtues we need, for example, for the gift of forgiveness, humility, charity, patience, faith, hope, or love. Jesus said: 'Ask, and it will be given you, seek, and you will find; knock, and it will be opened to you' (Luke 11:9). So we should go on asking for the virtues we need, believing not that we shall become perfect in this life, but that we shall by the grace of God grow in that direction.

Listening, discernment and words of knowledge

A major weakness in the life of prayer of many Christians is the failure to listen to God. Prayer should be a dialogue with God. All too easily it becomes a monologue, and God can hardly get a word in edgeways. The boy Samuel said: 'Speak, for thy servant hears' (1 Samuel 3:10). We often only say: 'Listen, Lord, your servant is speaking.'

Listening to God is especially important in praying for healing. If we do not learn to listen to God, we shall often not know what to pray for. We should listen not only to what the sick person has to say but also to what God is telling us – and the two do not always coincide. We should pray for the gift of discernment, for without it we shall sometimes misunderstand both the person and the situation, give unhelpful advice, and pray partly for the wrong things.

How do we listen to God? Place the sick person, their needs

and situation in God's hands, ask the Holy Spirit to enlighten us, and then listen, preferably in silence. God may answer in different ways. He may clarify our thinking processes so that a situation which seemed confused becomes clear. Or we may get a 'word' coming into our minds, for example, the word 'father', which might indicate that we should pray for someone's relationship with their father. Some people get mental pictures, which can give direction to their prayers. Needless to say such 'words' and 'pictures' or impressions are not infallible and have to be tested. But in my experience in our healing teams, these insights are normally of real help.

Some Christians with gifts of healing are given these 'words' – we usually call them 'words of knowledge' – in healing services. They will feel that God is healing or wanting to heal someone present with a particular complaint, such as a sick right knee, or lung trouble, or deafness in the left ear, or a bad back, or depression. When or if it is appropriate the person who receives the 'word' will announce it publicly, and frequently these 'words' are confirmed as the sick person in question makes him or herself known and if necessary comes forward to be prayed with for healing. Sometimes the person who has been given the 'word of knowledge' also receives additional precise information about the sick person in question, for instance their age or work. I remember one 'word of knowledge' in our Cockfosters' prayer group in which it was said that a person with a particular sickness worked with legal documents – and this was confirmed later.

'Words of knowledge' are not limited to the realm of healing. A 'word of knowledge' was once given out in our Cockfosters' prayer group saying that someone present who was experiencing a sensation in their right thumb and forefinger was intending to refuse to undertake some task, but that God wanted them to accept it. There was present a woman who had been invited by her parish priest to become an extraordinary minister of communion. She had said 'Yes' to the invitation, but on returning home she had had second thoughts and had decided to return to the priest to tell him that she had changed her mind. As this 'word' was being given out she was feeling a sensation in her right thumb and forefinger – which one uses of course for giving out communion. So she recognized that God was speaking to her through this 'word of knowledge', and today she is an extraordinary minister of communion.

How do people with this gift receive a 'word of knowledge' for physical healing? There are several ways. For physical sickness the most common way is probably that of feeling a pain or sensation in one's own body when God wants to heal someone else with a sickness in the same part of their body. So receiving a pain or sensation in one's left hand could indicate that God is wanting to heal or is healing someone's left hand. Another way is the receiving of a mental picture of a part of the body which God is healing or wants to heal in someone. A third way is through a word or sentence coming into one's mind, for instance, 'left elbow' or 'arthritis in the left elbow'.

An increasing number of Christians seem to be receiving the gift of 'words of knowledge'. What are we to think of this? Since many people are clearly being helped and healed by Jesus through the exercise of this gift, we obviously should in general welcome it - and even in a guarded way encourage its wider use. However it is very important that at the same time it should be carefully tested and exercised under control. Only people with a tested and approved gift of the 'word of knowledge' should be allowed to exercise it in healing services or sessions, for mistaken or unwisely used 'words of knowledge' can do real harm.

With what words should we pray? Passages of Scripture

Basically, we should pray with the words the Holy Spirit leads us to use – and no two people will be led in exactly the same way. There are no magical formulas. Having said that, we can however make certain general suggestions.

As I wrote earlier, it is good to start with praise and a prayer for protection. This can be followed by repentance for we are all sinners and we all need to come before God in repentance.

Failure to repent can block the healing power of Jesus for he answers the prayers of the humble not the proud. The person, their sickness and circumstances can be offered to God, asking that his perfect will may be done in them. I often follow this with the Our Father, where we say 'Your will be done on earth as it is in heaven'. Then one can pray that God will bless and heal the sick person. This can be followed by praise; indeed it is good to intersperse praise and thanksgiving throughout the healing session.

When praying for healing it can be good to use a number of set prayers like the Our Father and the Hail Mary (for Catholics), or any other set prayer which is found helpful. I would, however, also encourage people to try to pray spontaneously, simply speaking as the Holy Spirit leads them. Some Catholics are not used to this, and feel that their own words lack dignity or literary excellence or theological precision. But our prayers are not going to be answered because of their literary excellence or theological development, but because they come from the heart and are said with faith. When we speak to our own human father or brother we do not feel that we have to bother about using refined English. It should be the same when we are praying to our Heavenly Father and to our brother Jesus. The right prayer may simply be: 'Jesus, mercy'; 'Father, please help and heal'; 'Come Holy Spirit'; 'Our Lady, pray for healing'; 'Thank you God'; 'Alleluia, alleluia, alleluia'. Usually the simpler the prayer the better.

People who have the gift of tongues will usually use it much during a healing session, for it can be a great help when praying for healing. Indeed I personally would find it difficult to pray over someone for healing without praying in tongues. However, praying aloud in tongues could be off-putting for people not used to it. So I often pray over a sick person silently in tongues rather than aloud. It is also important to add that people without this gift are not thereby 'second class citizens' in the healing ministry. I know people with very powerful healing ministries who do not speak in tongues – and I do not think Padre Pio spoke in tongues. However, I also know people whose healing ministries increased in power greatly when they received the gift of tongues.

There should also usually be periods of silence when we are praying for healing. We normally need times of quiet to wait on the Lord and listen to him. 'And in praying do not heap up empty phrases as the Gentiles do; for they think that they will be heard for their many words' (Matthew 6:7). The healing ministry of quite a few people would gain if they gave a greater place to silence and to the listening which goes with it.

Some Christians when praying for healing pray especially to the Father, for example, Monsignor Michael Buckley who has written very beautifully about this in his excellent book, *His Healing Touch* (Collins, Fount Paperbacks 1987). Other people tend to pray more directly to Jesus – I include myself in this group. John Wimber and those who have been influenced by his style of ministry tend to call much on the Holy Spirit to come, which I increasingly do myself. (Of course they all pray to Father, Son and Holy Spirit. But there can be different emphases.) In this matter I think Christians should pray as the Holy Spirit leads them, but all will normally want to bring into their prayer the Father, Jesus and the Holy Spirit.

Catholics will also surely want to ask Our Lady, the saints and the angels to pray for the healing of the sick – I myself always like to include a prayer to Our Lady. However, this should remain definitely secondary to praying to the three divine persons. And it is good to remember the words of Our Lady in Medjugorje who said that it is Jesus not she who heals. Our Lady herself is not pleased if we try more or less to put her on the same level as Jesus.

It is usually good to read one or more passages from the Bible, for example, Psalm 51 (50) for repentance, Psalm 23 (22) for hope, or a psalm of praise like Psalm 145. Another very helpful practice is to read an account of one of Jesus' healing miracles, choosing one which is particularly suitable for the person in question, e.g. the healing of blind Bartimaeus (Mark 10:46ff) for a person with eye trouble.

Sacred Scripture is a special channel of healing power, and

it is important if possible to encourage sick people to get to know and love the Bible. Indeed, learning passages of the Bible by heart can be a great help to sick people.

A number of years ago now a man came to see me with a very bad breakdown. I prayed with him frequently over a considerable period, and I gave him a list of passages from the Bible, some of which I suggested he might find helpful to read from time to time. To my surprise, he started reading them all every day, and he kept this up for a few years. He called the passages 'My Office'. In fact, after a time he could recite most of them by heart. I am sure that this daily Bible reading played an important part in his recovery. Although he is now no longer ill, he still reads or recites some of these passages regularly.

(For anyone who is interested, the following were the passages I gave him, as far as I can remember: Psalms 130 (129); 51 (50); 23 (22); 121 (120); 100 (99); 148; 149 and 150; Matthew 6:25–34; 8:14–17; 11:28–30; Mark 10:46–52; Luke 11:5–13; Romans 8:28–39; 1 Peter 5:6–7.)

When I pray for healing I normally pray for the healing of spirit and mind before I pray for the healing of the body. I often ask Jesus to fill the whole person with the healing light of his love. And I wait as I see or imagine with my mind's eye, so to speak, the healing light of Jesus filling the person, and especially filling any part of the body which is sick. However it is important to say that healings are not dependent on our feelings or imaginings. Sometimes when all I am feeling is tiredness, unbelief, unworthiness and the desire to finish the healing session quickly more healing seems to happen! Jesus is Lord. And healings take place when and how he wishes, not when we feel great or on form!

It can be good also to rebuke the sickness. I often say: 'In the name of Jesus Christ I rebuke this sickness (of the eyes, or leg, or depression, or whatever). Be healed.' We read of Jesus in Luke 4:39 that 'he stood over her and rebuked the fever, and it left her'. It can help sometimes to take authority firmly over a sickness and rebuke it in the name of Jesus.

I also normally ask someone I am praying with whether

they feel anything. They quite often say that they are feeling peaceful, perhaps very peaceful. They may also say that they feel they are experiencing warmth or heat going through their whole body or through the part of the body which is being prayed over. They also sometimes talk of tingling or glowing sensations or an electric-like force going through them. Occasionally they say they are feeling cold or that a part of their body feels cold. They often say that they feel nothing. They may very occasionally even say that they feel worse!

Sensations and feelings of the kind described above can help to guide us in our praying with people. For instance if someone feels nothing in their right knee when I pray over it and considerable heat in their left knee, then I will probably concentrate my praying on the left knee, since more seems to be happening there. However, it is important not to attach too much significance to feelings and sensations, or to become too fascinated by them. People can be healed while feeling nothing. And people can remain sick after experiencing much heat or other sensations. As to those who say that they feel worse, sometimes a sharper physical pain is a sign that healing is taking place. Usually the pain disappears or diminishes after a moment.

Laying hands on the sick

Jesus frequently laid hands on the sick when he healed them.

And some people brought to him a blind man, and begged him to touch him. And he took the blind man by the hand, and led him out of the village; and when he had spit on his eyes and laid his hands upon him, he asked him, 'Do you see anything?' And he looked up and said: 'I see men, but they look like trees, walking.' Then again he laid his hands upon his eyes; and he looked intently and was restored, and saw everything clearly. (Mark 8:22–5)

Jesus also encouraged his disciples to lay their hands on the sick: 'And these signs will accompany those who believe . . .

they will lay their hands on the sick, and they will recover'
(Mark 16:17). This is what we find happening in the Acts of
the Apostles: 'Now many signs and wonders were done among
the people by the hands of the apostles' (Acts 5:12). 'So they
(Paul and Barnabas) remained for a long time, speaking boldly
for the Lord, who bore witness to the word of his grace, grant-
ing signs and wonders to be done by their hands' (Acts 14:3).
'It happened that the father of Publius lay sick with fever and
dysentery; and Paul visited him and prayed, and putting his
hands on him healed him' (Acts 28:8).

Laying hands on the sick is not only following the New
Testament practice. It is also a natural human reaction. If a
child bangs his or her knee the mother will often spontaneously
put her hand on the hurting knee. Indeed a person who has
banged their knee will frequently put their own hands on it.
For whatever reason the laying of a hand on a hurting knee or
on a feverish brow can be a help. It is of course an expression
of sympathy, but there seems to be more in it than that.

In the United States this practice of the laying on of hands
has been developed in the secular field of professional nursing.
Dolores Kreigger Ph.D., R.N. has written a book, *The Therapeutic Touch. How to use your hands to help or heal* (Prentice
Hall, Inc., Englewood Cliffs, N.J., 07632, 1979). In this book
she describes the beneficial effects of this practice on patients
and how she has trained large numbers of nurses in it. In some
American hospitals the doctors will order therapeutic touch as
a treatment to be given to a patient and the nurses will carry
it out as they would other prescribed treatments.

Many Christians involved in praying for healing have found
that often more healing happens when they follow the New
Testament practice of the laying on of hands. It is especially
when hands are laid on that sick people experience such things
as the healing heat mentioned in the last section. Indeed, not
being able to lay on hands can be something of a barrier to
being able to help someone.

It is normally good to lay hands on the head of a sick person,
either standing behind them or to the side of them. Or if

this would be rather off-putting one can simply take hold of someone's hand or hands, or put one's hand on their shoulder.

Experience shows that it is usually good when possible to place the hand on the sick part of the body – as Jesus laid his hands on the eyes of the blind man in the quotation from Mark 8 above. It is not of course necessary to place the hand on the skin of the sick person. If I am praying for an arthritic shoulder I would normally ask someone to take off their jacket or coat, but this would be enough.

Needless to say, it is important not to embarrass the sick person, and the person praying for healing needs to be sensitive in this matter. It is also essential not to give people an opportunity for gossip. Perhaps partly for these reasons, some Christians in the healing ministry place their hands near the sick person rather than on them. Doubtless this can be the right thing to do in some circumstances, but I personally prefer to follow the New Testament practice of laying hands on the sick rather than near the sick. If a woman has an illness of the abdomen or a cancer in the breast, a man praying for healing can ask the woman to place her own hands over the sick part and can place his hand over hers. Obviously it is important to avoid anything unseemly.

The healing of life-styles

Frequently people are suffering from an illness because in one or more ways their life-style is very unwise. It may be a matter of smoking, alcoholism, or other drugs, over-eating, or eating the wrong things, being a workaholic, lack of exercise or sleep, sexual indulgences or unnecessary stress. In these cases it is obviously not enough to pray for the healing of the physical illness – one needs also to pray for the healing of the life-style. So if someone is suffering from a bad chest and smoking forty cigarettes per day, clearly one needs to pray also for the healing of addiction to nicotine – and for healing of the inner hurts which may lie behind the addiction – and perhaps also for the healing of the whole situation in which the person is involved.

All this will sometimes necessitate a certain amount of counselling. It is surprising how frequently even otherwise intelligent people are blind to the obviously harmful effects of their lifestyles on their health. I know of a man at the top of his profession in England who kids himself, so I am told, that there is no connection between his chain-smoking and the rapidly deteriorating condition of his lungs. It is surprising also how many people who are clearly overdrinking pretend that their consumption of alcohol is quite reasonable.

There is surely something wrong in a person asking God to heal their illnesses and not trying to do anything about healing the bad life-style which causes them. Healing miracles are not meant to be a substitute for sound living. I think the whole area of diet is a field in which this obviously applies. Many people are overeating or eating and drinking the wrong things – and making no or little effort to change these habits.

I have in front of me a *Guide to Healthy Eating*, produced by the Health Education Council and distributed freely by our local borough. Right at the front of the guide it makes the following five points, which are developed in the rest of the booklet: 'Cut down on fat, sugar and salt; Eat more fibre-rich foods; Eat plenty of fresh fruit and vegetables; Go easy on alcohol; Get plenty of variety in what you eat.' How many people are simply ignoring the advice contained in this booklet? How many priests are probably shortening the length of their active ministry by eating too much or the wrong things and by not taking enough exercise? Only yesterday I was speaking with a priest under sixty whose health has cracked up because, so he told me, he was over-active and ate unwisely. Why wait until one has had a stroke or a heart attack before eating sensibly and taking enough exercise? I know a priest who had to have open-heart surgery when he was about sixty. Now he lives a rigorous life of no smoking, and carefully planned diet and exercise. What a pity he did not get on to a healthy regime before he had the heart attack!

Health is a great gift from God. To live healthily as far as we reasonably can is surely an expression of gratitude to God and an expression of the right kind of self-love. Obviously it is right sometimes to risk or sacrifice it for a good cause, as many missionaries have done. Also we must avoid an excessive concern for our health. But to neglect or abuse our health unnecessarily is not pleasing to the God who created us, and gave it to us.

Living healthily involves being disciplined and making sacrifices and can be, I think, a very suitable form of asceticism in our age. There is a Benedictine monastery at Pecos in the USA where all the monks and sisters are involved in the Charismatic Renewal and where no one smokes and where the community's life-style in matters of food, drink and exercise are very much on health-building lines. I was very impressed by all this when I was there, and I think this life-style helps in part to explain why this community is so very fruitful as a centre for retreats and for the healing ministry.

So, to conclude, I think that our work in the healing ministry of prayer will quite often involve us in praying for the healing of bad life-styles, for people to give up smoking and excessive drinking, for people to eat wisely and take enough exercise and rest, for people to stop worshipping mammon and overworking in the pursuit of wealth – and sometimes it will perhaps involve us in giving someone a copy of a *Guide to Healthy Eating*!

6

Praying For Healing • II

Praying for your own healing

Not infrequently I meet Catholics who are ill, sometimes seriously, who have never prayed for their own physical healing.
When asked why they give various reasons. Some will reply
that other people are more ill or needy than they are and that
it is more important to pray for these others. This argument
seems to presuppose a limited God who can only answer a
certain number of prayers, so that if I receive some of his
healing love he will have less to give others. The correct
response is that God is infinite and that my receiving of his
healing love does not mean that he has less for others. I can
pray both for my own healing and that of other people.

Some Christians, especially perhaps some Catholics, do not
pray for their own physical healing because they think it is
nobler and less selfish to accept the cross of sickness sent by
the Lord and offer it up rather than pray for physical healing.
Leaving aside special cases where the Holy Spirit himself leads
a particular person not to pray for physical healing, perhaps
for example a very elderly person who rightly feels that God
is now calling them to himself in heaven, I think this attitude
is in general wrong – and for various reasons.

In the first place, I do not believe that God normally sends
people sickness, although he certainly allows people to become
ill and will often bring good out of a sickness. Indeed, the devil
not infrequently plays his part in making people sick so that
they cannot do the work God wanted them to do. For example,

if a parish priest becomes unwell there will sometimes be no Mass on Sunday in the parish.

Secondly, we have in general a moral obligation to try to be in good health, so that we can serve God more actively and are less trouble to other people. If I fall and break my wrist, then I have a moral obligation to try to get it healed, normally by going to the doctor – and, I would think, also through prayer. To justify not going to the doctor by saying that if I do not seek medical attention I will have more suffering and sickness in my wrist to offer up would clearly be wrong.

We have in general a moral obligation to make use of medical science – or some alternative therapy – in order to try to be in good health. I would suggest that in the same way we should usually make use of prayer for healing. It is no more selfish to pray for one's physical healing than it is to go to the doctor. In both cases we are seeking to be well so that we can serve God more actively and be less trouble to others. I would add that seeking to be or remain in good health is surely also part of the commandment to love ourselves. Some Christians seem to believe that Jesus said: 'You shall love your neighbour and not yourself' instead of 'You shall love your neighbour as yourself' (Matthew 22:39).

Other Christians say that they do not pray for their own physical well-being because the only thing that really matters is spiritual health. Is it not better to concentrate on the important and leave aside the unimportant? It is of course in general of greater value to pray for our spiritual health rather than our physical health. But we can pray for both. My main answer to this objection is that it makes complete nonsense of the healing ministry of Jesus and the apostles, who went round healing bodies as well as souls. Let us not try to be more spiritual than Jesus, who was very interested in healing bodies!

Finally, some Christians do not pray for their physical healing because they do not feel worthy to do so, because they feel that they have done nothing to deserve the healing touch of Jesus, because their weak prayers in any case would not make any difference. The answer to these objections is that Jesus came to save and heal sinners not 'good' people who do not need forgiveness. So if we repent of our sins he will forgive us and we can pray to him for healing. It is not a question of deserving to be healed, or being a great prayer. The healing touch of Jesus is all love, mercy, forgiveness, grace, undeserved blessing. So any repentant sinner – and that should be all of us – can turn to Jesus with hope for healing. People are healed by Jesus not because they are worthy but because he is worthy!

Praying for one's own healing is very much like praying for someone else's. When I receive communion I ask Jesus to fill me with his healing love, spirit, mind and body, praying especially for any particular healing of spirit, mind or body of which I become aware. I ask Jesus to fill me with the healing light of his love. I also sometimes ask the Holy Spirit to fill me with his healing presence. I also ask Our Lady, the saints and the angels to pray for or watch over my health. If I am praying for a sick part of my body, I will normally lay my hands on it, praying both in English and in tongues, and thinking of that part of the body as being filled with the healing light of Jesus. I also rebuke the sickness in the name of Jesus. And I will often anoint the sick part of my body with the sacramental of blessed oil.

Perhaps I may be allowed to testify here. During the Second World War I was knocked over by a car and my left ankle was broken. The bones set wrongly, and about fifteen years later I began to limp badly. A top surgeon then performed a lengthy operation. After this I no longer limped, but if I ran for a bus I would almost certainly find myself limping afterwards. As the years went by I would sometimes limp when walking. My local doctor could do nothing for me. I then started asking people to pray over my ankle and this helped. But what was especially beneficial was when I started placing my hands on my ankle and praying over it – usually in tongues – for about thirty seconds every night, also anointing it with blessed oil – all of which I still do. I now normally (at the age of sixty-seven) do a very short jog every morning – something my ankle could not stand up to for many years. Recently when I showed it to a Catholic doctor who I was seeing about someone else's health, he was amazed that I could walk and run as I do with an ankle which is as discoloured and deformed as mine is – he said he would have expected me to be walking with a stick.

Yes, we are in general right to pray for our own healing, including physical healing. And if we do so our body is likely to be in better health than if we do not pray for it. However, this prayer should be against a background of handing our health entirely over to God and saying 'Yes' to whatever his will for us is, including any trial of sickness. And I must add that we should try to avoid any excessive preoccupation with our own health.

One last point: people can be healed in answer to prayer without praying for their own healing. However, Jesus does seem quite often to wait for someone to start praying for their own healing before he heals them. Doubtless there will be some readers of this book whose healing will be delayed until they start praying for it themselves. So why not try praying for it right now?

Healing prayer for the elderly and the dying

When we pray for healing for the elderly, what are we praying for? Obviously we pray for spiritual healing and for the healing of things like fears, anxieties, depression, the difficult memories of the past. All this will largely be the subject of the next chapter. But what are we praying for when we pray for physical healing? As the years go by inevitably our bodies begin to wear out, our eyes see less well, we hear less easily, our backs get stiffer, we find it more difficult to move about – we might say that the 'ageing car' begins to rattle in various places! Do we pray that an elderly person will have the sight and hearing, mobility and strength of a teenager? Obviously it would be unrealistic and out of place to ask God to give someone advanced in years the body of a teenager again. However, it is possible for people to grow old in a more gentle and unbroken way, more able to cope physically with life; or it can be in a more broken, disrupted way, less able to cope physically and more dependent on the help of others. We can pray that the former way of growing old comes to pass, that eyesight, hearing and mobility will last longer, that the mind will remain clear, that the ageing person will be able to cope in a way that is less burdensome to others.

Praying for the healing of parts of the body like eyes, ears, backs and chests in elderly people can be very worthwhile even if there is no actual improvement. Prayer can be used by God to slow down the rate of deterioration, to help parts of the body to last out longer.

However that does not mean that we should not hope to see physical improvements in answer to prayers for older people. I remember Winifred in our prayer group whom the doctor had given three months to live with cancer when she was in her seventies. After prayer most of the cancer disappeared to the amazement of the consultant, and Winifred spent the next six years free from trouble with cancer. It is worth adding that her husband of about the same age received a healing of arthritis in his knee on the first evening they came to our prayer group, which was a big help in enabling him to support his wife. (The two of them came with and at the suggestion of Winifred's former doctor.)

Quite often when we pray for physical healing with elderly people – indeed with other people also – there is a temporary improvement and then things return to their former state or continue to deteriorate. In these cases I start by thanking God for the temporary improvement in healing. Thank God if the pain disappeared or was reduced for only a few hours; thank God if someone had one good night's sleep.

For some time I was praying regularly with an aged aunt of mine who suffered from a number of physical illnesses. Amongst these was a sick foot which made walking painful and difficult. There was always an improvement in the foot after we had prayed – less pain and she could walk more easily. But when I saw her again about two weeks later, the foot was back where it had been – indeed there was a downward trend. Some people may think that this praying for her foot was a waste of time. But I have often reflected that if we had not prayed for the foot, she might well have spent the last year of her life in bed instead of only the last three months as actually happened. I must add of course that physical healing was not the most important thing we prayed for.

Perhaps I may be allowed also to refer to my experience of praying for healing for my beloved father and mother who died at the age of ninety-three and ninety-four respectively. They were very generously and imaginatively cared for by my sister with whom they were living during the last years of their lives. She also prayed for their healing. My father published his book of poems at the age of eighty-seven, and my mother read a lesson in church and tobogganed on ice at the age of ninety-four – and beat me at a game of scrabble five weeks before she died. For years I prayed for my father's eyes (glaucoma and later also cataract) and my mother's hearing, that they would last out until my parents passed on to the fuller life – and they did last out, but only just! For a long time the eye specialist expressed surprise that my father's eyes deteriorated so slowly. Then, to the specialist's very great amazement, my father's eyes improved considerably when he was about ninety-one, so that afterwards he only had to visit the specialist every six months instead of every three. His eyes began to deteriorate again later, but that very unexpected, sudden improvement probably resulted in my father being able to see until the end of his life. I write this to show that we should never assume that God is not going to do remarkable physical healings for the very elderly, that we should go on praying for the healing of physical infirmities.

My parents both suffered from a number of physical infirmities in their last years. When I prayed for the healing of their ailments, for example, my mother's arthritis and my father's heart, I would tell them that I was not praying that they would live for a day longer than God wanted – and they both understood this. In fact the three of us prayed that God would take us at the right moment and prepare us for that time.

My father died after three weeks in hospital and my mother after three days in a nursing home. In God's providence they both died when they did largely, I think, because they knew it was time to go, and they did not wish to be a burden to others. I telephoned the nursing home on the evening my mother died and I was told that she was declining but that the doctor had said that day there was no immediate danger of death. Immediately after telephoning I celebrated a house Mass, and we prayed that the Lord would come soon for my mother – and he did. My brother telephoned immediately after the Mass to say that she had died.

Sometimes people are clinging on to life when it is time to leave this earth. They may be holding on because of fear of death, fear of judgement, the need to be reconciled to someone, the need to communicate something or to do something. They have in one way or another some unfinished business to do before they are ready to go. Our task can be through prayer and in other ways to help them to complete their business so that they can pass on to the fuller life. (There is an excellent book on this subject by Mary Jane Linn csj, Dennis Linn sj and Matthew Linn sj: *Healing the Dying*, Paulist Press, New York, 1979.)

So it can sometimes be right to pray, as I did for my mother: 'Jesus, please come and take this person soon.' This prayer can be especially appropriate when someone is suffering much. Praying for healing will sometimes result in someone dying sooner rather than living longer. We need to remember that none of us will be fully healed until we get to heaven. We should not seek to delay the ultimate healing when the time for it has come.

Most healing is gradual

Most healing in answer to prayer is gradual, whether it is healing of spirit, mind or body. Immediate healings are more rare, especially when the sickness is serious. This means that there is normally need for ongoing prayer for healing.

We usually suggest to sick people who come to our healing services or sessions that they should come back for further ministry, perhaps come along regularly for quite a time. If we pray with someone for depression or arthritis and there is some improvement, it is probable that if they return for prayer the following week there will be a further improvement. Moreover, if they do not seem to have benefited the first time, they may begin to improve on the second or third or tenth visit.

I remember the case of a woman in her thirties who came for prayer especially for her physical health, there being several parts of her body causing her trouble. We prayed on about six occasions for all her physical ailments but none of them seemed to improve, though she was experiencing great spiritual blessings. Eventually on about the seventh visit her knee was healed, and after that other parts began to improve. Now this person is one of the leaders of one of our healing teams. If this woman had given up coming after the fifth visit, assuming that no physical healing was going to happen – or if we on the healing team had given up praying for her physical healing – then she would have missed what God had in store for her through our ministry.

There are some people who have been coming to our healing sessions for quite a time, even a few years, to be prayed with for the same things, and apparently there is no improvement. I think of a person with deep depression, of another with deep fears, of another with arthritic shoulders, of another person who is an alcoholic. Is our ministry here a waste of time, as some people have suggested? I do not believe so, although obviously it feels more rewarding for a member of a healing team to see healings happening. It may be however that our regular ministry has prevented the depression or other sickness from getting worse. It may also be that our regular prayer has helped to keep the person's head above water. Or it may be that God has used it to bless someone in another direction. The person with deep fears mentioned above says that her moments of fear have not improved. She has however now been baptized as a Catholic and her husband has started going to communion again after many years. As to the alcoholic mentioned above, he still drinks and the general state of his health has declined. But he has come back to the sacraments with real sincerity after being away for many years.

Francis MacNutt taught us the importance of ongoing praying for healing, of 'soaking prayer' as he called it. This can apply not only to the number of healing prayer sessions, but also to their length. Sometimes there have been remarkable results when prayer for physical healing was continued by a healing team for several hours on end. If someone is moving an arthritic limb more easily after ten minutes' prayer, it is probable that they will move it still more easily after a further ten minutes or still longer. All this poses problems of time and energy for those ministering healing prayer. There is need for the gift of discernment and the light of the Holy Spirit in knowing how often and for how long to pray with a sick person – and this also for the sake of the person concerned who must not become overtired.

A last point: since most healing is gradual, it is often desirable if possible to arrange for a follow-up session. This may simply be a matter of arranging to see the person again at the prayer meeting the following week. Or it may be desirable to take the person's telephone number and address, or give them one's own. If the ministry is mainly for an arthritic elbow, we may not need to do this. If, however, one is praying with a depressed and suicidal person, it can be very necessary to keep in contact if possible. And if circumstances prevent this because, for example, one is only visiting the district, then it is important to try to put the person in contact with a suitable local Christian. Indeed it could be a mistake to start certain forms of healing ministry if one is not able to follow it up or arrange for someone else to do so.

Praying for healing on the telephone

More and more Christians are finding that praying for healing over the telephone can be very worthwhile. Obviously it is

normally better to pray in the presence of the sick person but
it is not always possible for one reason or another. Praying for
healing on the telephone can be more effective than simply
praying for the absent person; it often seems to add something
to absent prayers.

I find myself praying for healing on the telephone very frequently. It may be that a depressed person or a sufferer from
cancer telephones me and asks to come and see me. After
fixing an appointment I often suggest that we say a short prayer,
and this frequently seems to bring real help. Or it may be
someone whom I have prayed over in a prayer group or at the
monastery, and we follow this up by praying together on the
telephone. Perhaps someone lives too far away for us to be
able to arrange a meeting, or someone is going through a time
of immediate crisis or special difficulty. And of course one is
not only asked to pray for healing on the telephone: a lady
used to phone me from the USA to ask me to pray for her
matrimonial problems. She once asked me to pray for her
financial difficulties, which I did – but I think I also suggested
that seeing or telephoning someone living near her would be
cheaper!

When it comes to praying on the telephone I am not only
on the giving end. If I have a special problem or if I feel that
I am being threatened by 'flu, for example, I may well phone
a member of our healing team and ask them to pray with me.

When praying for a physical sickness on the telephone it is
good to ask the sick person to put their free hand on the part
of their body which is affected if this is possible. It is also in
general helpful to pray for quite a time if convenient – and if
one's telephone bill can stand it!

Members of our healing teams have sometimes seen remarkable results from praying for healing in this way. There was
the sister who began to see more clearly through her bad eye
as she was being prayed with for healing on the telephone.
Another person felt her deep depression being lifted as she was
prayed for. People not infrequently feel a healing warmth in
the sick parts of their body when being prayed with on the

phone. And most obviously they often experience real peace as the prayer for healing continues.

One word of caution: I think that prayer for healing over the telephone should normally be kept simple. Praying for deep inner healing and especially praying for deliverance could open up wounds which really require the physical presence of the person giving the ministry.

A last point: praying for healing on the telephone can cause a real problem for some members of healing teams: the telephone can ring so often that the situation gets out of hand. One priest with a powerful ministry of healing had to run off to the USA for some months to avoid the deluge of telephone calls. A married woman had to change her telephone number twice. Members of healing teams may need to think and pray before giving people their telephone numbers. They may also sometimes just need to leave the phone ringing, while saying a quick prayer for whoever may be on the other end of the line. I do not think that God always wants us to answer the phone. Some of us need to pray about when and when not to answer. The writing of this book has meant that a considerable number of telephone calls have gone unanswered.

Confidentiality

Members of praying for healing teams and other individuals involved in this ministry will frequently be told things which people may normally only tell doctors, nurses or the clergy. Obviously they need to observe the same rules of confidentiality as the clergy and the medical profession do.

However, in our prayer groups sick people will often spontaneously share their problems, and this can be helpful from the point of view of encouraging and helping other people to pray for them – but sharing in public should have its limits!

Here in Cockfosters we have in addition to the large Monday evening prayer group, a smaller prayer group of about thirty people on Wednesday afternoons where there is much praying for healing and where the Lord has been doing beautiful things, including some helpful physical healing. The regulars at this meeting have become a very caring, loving group, and they will spontaneously share much with each other, thus enabling them to 'bear one another's burdens' (Galatians 6:2) in prayer. Only two weeks ago a lady who recently started coming for prayer after a cancer operation asked us all to pray for her husband who has a drinking problem. Last week she came back with a large smile on her face saying that for the first time for years her husband had not had a drink that week. Doubtless that change would not have happened if she had not felt able to share the problem.

I think all Christians should if possible be members of a small sharing group in which people support each other in prayer. However, sharing in a group needs to be accompanied by a sense of discretion and confidentiality, something for which we should pray.

'Resting in the Spirit'

Being a rather cautious person temperamentally, I would have preferred to write nothing about 'resting in the Spirit' in this book, for what I write is bound to be misunderstood by some people. However, I feel it would not be right to side-step a subject which is undoubtedly relevant, especially since some people may unexpectedly come across this phenomenon and wonder what is happening.

When prayed with for healing or for another purpose some people sometimes 'rest in the Spirit' or are 'overcome in the Spirit' or are 'slain in the Spirit', to use the names which are frequently, if not entirely happily, used for this experience. The person can appear to faint or nearly faint while in fact remaining conscious. They may fall to the floor or go limp in their chair. And this can last from a few seconds to several hours, although the latter is not common. Although this experience usually happens when people have hands laid on them in prayer, it can also occur without anyone being touched, especially in the setting of powerful worship.

There is no doubt whatever that a considerable number of people have received wonderful healings of spirit, mind or body and remarkable spiritual blessings while they 'rested in the Spirit'. I myself have been blessed in this way. In 1975 when Francis MacNutt prayed over me in a healing service I 'rested in the Spirit' for two hours and twenty minutes. During that time I not only realized that I had not forgiven certain people, a fact I was unaware of before, but I also learned more about the nature and demands of Christian forgiveness while lying on the ground there than I had ever understood from talks or books. The Holy Spirit gave me a much deeper insight on this subject, which I regard as one of the major spiritual blessings of my life.

I have also received significant blessings while 'resting in the Spirit' on three other occasions. Two of these experiences led me directly to undertake international journeys which were truly fruitful and blessed. The third experience was for me an important spiritual blessing which remains with me to this day.

So if people can benefit in this way by 'resting in the Spirit', why not simply rejoice and encourage this experience whenever possible? The answer is that although this experience can bring great blessings, it can also have its dangers, as Francis MacNutt pointed out in a chapter on this subject in his book, *The Power to Heal* (Ave Maria Press 1977), and as Cardinal Suenens has underlined in his book, *Resting in the Spirit* (Veritas 1987).

The dangers or problems can include:

(1) Sensationalism – people wanting to see lots of bodies falling around at a healing service or wanting to receive an emotional kick themselves.

(2) 'Resting in the Spirit' is not always only or mainly the work of the Holy Spirit – other factors can be involved.

(3) Pride – my own satisfaction at seeing people 'rest in the Spirit' when I prayed over them has not always been entirely of God.

(4) 'Resting in the Spirit' can open up deep inner wounds or spark off deliverance problems.

Father Leo Thomas OP in the chapter on this subject in his valuable book, *The Healing Team* (Paulist Press, 1987), writes: 'I view "resting in the Spirit" as a valuable aid to healing to be used only privately . . . I believe "resting in the Spirit" should *not* be used in large public gatherings. The person "resting in the Spirit" may need personal attention which cannot be given in mass meetings' (page 165).

In general I agree with Father Thomas. However one cannot of course always prevent people from 'resting in the Spirit' in large meetings. But one can influence the situation cconsiderably by the way the healing team prays over people. If they are prayed over while standing up, then far more are likely to fall to the ground 'resting in the Spirit'. If they are prayed over sitting on a chair, then far fewer are likely to 'rest in the Spirit', and those who do so will usually just slump back on the chair and not fall to the ground. When I am in charge of a public healing service I ask the healing team to use chairs if possible for those being prayed over, to avoid the problems which can arise when people fall to the ground right, left and centre. Although the faith of some will be strengthened by the sight of people falling down and 'resting in the Spirit' at healing services, others will be frightened and badly put off.

So I think it is in general better to pray with people sitting down in public healing services, but I would not want to criticize the ministry of someone like Father Edward McDonagh CSSR of Boston, who seems to have been led by God to pray with people standing up in his very powerful healing ministry. I also think that, in general, it is better to pray with people sitting down in smaller groups and on a one-to-one basis.

A further point: I think that Cardinal Suenens and John Richards are right when they point out the ambiguity of using the expression 'resting in the Spirit'. The 'resting' may not always be in the Spirit, it can be just an expression of human emotion. So if we do use this terminology, which seems to be widespread, let us not lose our sense of discernment.

A final warning: if you are praying with someone standing up, try to have a suitable person behind them to catch them if they fall. Otherwise stand by their side so that you yourself can catch them. And I add that I myself would never want to risk someone with a bad back problem falling down.

Healing services

Some Catholics query the need for healing services. They would say that every authentic Christian service of worship, especially every prayerful celebration of the Mass, is a healing event. So why talk about 'healing services' and 'healing Masses'? They might add that praying with people for healing is surely better done in private.

It is true that every authentic service of worship and every prayerful celebration of Mass is a healing event. There is however room for, indeed a need for, services of worship and celebrations of Mass which underline and give greater prominence to the healing side of prayer. There is, I think, a parallel with Masses specially celebrated for the intention of peace. At every mass we pray for peace; in some celebrations of the Mass we concentrate especially on praying for peace.

As to the objection that it is better to pray for healing in private, I think it is not a question of either/or but of both/and. We certainly need to pray for healing with some people in private. But we also need healing services, for two reasons. Firstly, some people would be too shy to come for individual ministry, but they would be willing to slip into the back of a healing service unnoticed. Secondly, there are far too many needing prayer for healing to be able to see them all in individual sessions. If I speak to one person on the importance of forgiveness for twenty minutes, I can touch one life. If I preach to a congregation of three hundred on the importance of forgiveness, as I frequently do, I can reach far more people with the healing message of the gospel.

Healing services can take various forms, this depending largely on the circumstances. Obviously there are big advantages in praying for healing within or following the celebration of Mass. However, this may be ruled out by the absence of a priest, or for ecumenical reasons when a large proportion of those present at the service are not Catholics. Whatever form the healing service takes, it would seem that the following elements should normally be present: a time of praise and worship; the reading of Scripture; a time for teaching or preaching; a prayer of repentance; general prayers for the healing of spirits, minds and bodies; when possible the laying on of hands; and when possible an anointing with oil. It is good also to include a prayer for sick people not present.

The following passages from the New Testament can be suitable for reading in healing services: Matthew 8:14–17; 9:18–26; 15:21–31; 17:14–21; Mark 2:1–12; 7:31–7; 9:14–29; 10:46–52; Luke 7:1–10; 8:40–56; 9:1–6; 17:11–19; John 4:46–54; 9:1–12; Acts 3:1–10; 5:12–16; 8:4–8; Romans 8:35–9; 1 Corinthians 13:1–13.

For about eight years now a Central London prayer group has arranged a Healing Mass on the first Friday of the month. This attracts about three hundred people and has, I think, been very worthwhile. We start with the celebration of Mass, the homily of which is usually connected with healing. After the Mass a general prayer for the healing of spirits, minds and bodies is said by two or three people. This is followed by an opportunity for the laying on of hands by members of our healing team, which includes medical doctors. We have a two-tier system for this – those who only want a brief prayer go to one part of the hall, where they receive the laying on of hands by a member of the healing team, who will pray over them for about twelve seconds and then anoint them with the sacramental of blessed oil. Those who want a lengthier period of ministry go to another part of the hall, where one or more members of the healing team will minister to them for five minutes or more. The whole evening lasts two and a half hours, but those who want or need to leave earlier can of course do so. It is important in a healing service that a sick person should not have to stay too long.

Fasting

As John L. Mackenzie writes in his well-known *Dictionary of the Bible* under the heading 'Fast': 'Jesus supposes that his disciples will fast.' Jesus said: 'And when you fast' (Matthew 6:16), not if you fast. He also said: 'The days will come, when the bridegroom is taken away from them, and then they will fast' (Matthew 9:15 cf. also Mark 2:18ff and Luke 5:33ff).

In the New Testament church we see the disciples fasting: 'While they were worshipping the Lord and fasting, the Holy Spirit said: 'Set apart for me Barnabas and Saul for the work to which I have called them'. Then after fasting and praying they laid their hands on them and sent them off' (Acts 13:2). We also read: 'And when they [Paul and Barnabas] had appointed elders for them in every church, with prayer and fasting, they committed them to the Lord in whom they believed' (Acts 14:23).

Many Christians have found from experience that when praying for healing the following of the biblical and ancient tradition of fasting has added something to prayer. I remember a leader of a house church with a powerful ministry of healing telling me that he found that if he fasted from solid food all day before taking a healing service in the evening, he was usually more blessed with 'words of knowledge'. I know a woman who is very gifted in praying for healing who will always try to fast during the week if she is leading a healing service at the weekend, for she has discovered that fasting strengthens her healing ministry. I myself, although not one of the stronger brethren when it comes to fasting, normally decide to drop a meal before a healing service. I also prefer not to pray for healing with an individual soon after a meal.

There are many different forms and degrees of fasting from food and drink. I advise people not to do any fasting with which a doctor would not be happy. Doctors, however, would be delighted if many of us did far more fasting! It is a sobering thought that in a world in which large numbers of people are dying from starvation, many Christians in this country and others are shortening their lives by overeating. This, however, is not the right place to develop that important subject.

Fasting can vary from dropping this or that item of food or drink, for example, sugar, sweets, meat, alcohol or coffee (partial fasting), to going without all food and drink, though I personally would never advise people to go without all liquids for reasons of health. Fasting can be for part of a day to several days or longer. It can be a regular practice – like the American sister whom I met who took no solid food one day every week for the sake of Latin America, where she had been a missionary. Or it can be an occasional practice when a particular situation seems to call for it, for example, someone's health crisis. An increasing number of Catholics are practising the 'Medjugorje fast', which is fasting on Fridays on bread and water, as asked for by Our Lady for the intention of peace.

The important thing is not that we do this or that particular fast, but that we fast as the Holy Spirit leads us – and he will direct us in very different ways. One friend of mine fasted from all solid food for three days for the sake of a healing service we were doing in his parish. He found no difficulty in doing it, which for me confirmed that his fast was of God. However, it could be very wrong for another person to try to do a three-day fast.

I think that those of us who are particularly involved in praying for healing do especially need to consider what God is asking us to do in the way of fasting. I know that I myself can always find plenty of excuses for not fasting – my tiredness, my health, the weather, what others will think – but God does seem to be pointing me more in that direction. Perhaps I am not the only one!

The healing of the family

Frequently the health of an individual is closely linked with the atmosphere and situation within their family. So when praying for the healing of an individual we often need to pray for the healing of relations within the family and for the whole family situation.

When a husband and wife are both present it can frequently be good to pray over them together. I sometimes encourage them to hold hands and I ask Jesus to restore anything which needs healing in their relationship. I also pray that Jesus may be more and more at the centre of their marriage, that they may be more and more united in his love and light, that they may increasingly be led by the Holy Spirit in their relationship, that there may be perfect forgiveness, and that their union may be ever more fruitful for the building up of God's Kingdom. One can also pray for the children of the marriage.

In praying for these things it is important not to forget to thank God for all his past blessings on the marriage and the family.

7

Inner Healing and Forgiveness

When reflecting this morning on the writing of this chapter, I found myself thinking: 'What am I doing writing on this subject? People have been praying with me for inner healing since 1972, and I still suffer from anxiety, fears, guilt and anger. Who am I to write on this subject?' Then I realized with gratitude how much healing of anxiety, fears, guilt and anger had taken place in me since 1972. I also remembered that our inner healing will only be complete when we get to heaven. Finally, I was reminded that the most obvious way in which I personally am used in prayer by Jesus is in bringing people peace. Thousands of people have said after I have prayed with them that they experienced peace or sometimes great peace. Indeed, I have at times felt frustrated that there was apparently no physical healing after prayer, and I have had to remind myself that the peace they experienced was perhaps more important or at any rate what God wanted to do. (I once was invited to pray one morning with a married man in his fifties who was going to have a serious cancer operation in the afternoon. He died in or just after the operation, and I felt rather a failure. Some time later a priest who was a close friend of the man who had died thanked me warmly for my ministry to him. He said that his friend had been full of fear until we had prayed together. Afterwards he had felt full of peace and the fear had left him. So much for our impressions of when we have failed and when we have succeeded!)

Perhaps my qualifications for writing this chapter are largely that I have personally experienced much anxiety, fear, guilt and anger, and thus understand and sympathize with people with these problems, which are still mine to a much lesser extent. There is also the fact that Jesus seems to use me to heal anxiety, fear, guilt and anger and to bring his peace to people. (All this may be very relevant for quite a few readers who feel that their own need of inner healing means that they cannot be used by Jesus to heal other people. Jesus does not wait for his followers to be fully healed before he uses them to bring release to others!)

In his important book, *Power Healing* (Hodder and Stoughton, 1986, page 95), John Wimber defines inner healing as 'a process in which the Holy Spirit brings forgiveness of sins and emotional renewal to people suffering from damaged minds, wills and emotions'. In the very imperfect world in which we live we all suffer from 'damaged minds, wills and emotions', so we all need inner healing, though for some it is much more pressing than for others. I thank God that I was born into a truly loving and caring home and family – and I realize increasingly how much I should thank God for this inestimable blessing when I am ministering to people, as I frequently do, whose mothers tried to abort them, or who were physically and mentally ill-treated by their parents, or who were sexually abused as a child or adolescent, or who frequently saw their drunken father beating their mother, or whose mother and father did not speak to each other – alas, these situations are far more common than is usually imagined. However, even those of us who were very fortunate in being born into really loving homes were wounded in some ways. For instance, in my case my elder brother nearly died of chest trouble while my mother was carrying me, which naturally made my mother very anxious, and I was born one month early – all of which of course inevitably affected me.

We can be wounded from the moment of conception, for example, when it takes place as a result of a woman being raped. We can be wounded while we are in the womb, for the shocks and stresses experienced by the mother affect her child. We can be wounded at the time of our birth – the late Doctor Frank Lake used to think that claustrophobia later in life was frequently caused by difficult births. We can be wounded in infancy and childhood by such events as the death of our mother, father, brother or sister, by a motor car accident or fire, by economic hardship and financial crisis in the home, by our inability to learn to spell at school (that gave me night-mares), and by numerous apparently lesser events like the death of a dog. We can very obviously be wounded in ado-lescence as we try to cope with our developing sexuality and with the process of becoming an adult, or as we have to face the pressure of examinations. We can be wounded as adults when things go wrong in a marriage, when a child dies, when we cannot get a job, when our son or daughter takes to heroine, when our husband or wife dies or walks out, when we lose our sight. The list could be nearly endless.

What are we to do with these wounds? We can ask Jesus, who was present with us during each difficult experience – because he is always with us, loving us, caring for us, watching over us – to heal the wounds, to pour forth the balm of his healing love on our painful memories, to make up for any lack of love or understanding in the past on the part of our parents or other people, to supply whatever support and help were lacking. Catholics can also ask Our Lady to pray for the healing of these inner wounds, especially any caused by the absence of maternal love and understanding. We can ask her to be a spiritual mother for us and to make up for what was lacking in our earthly mother - perhaps unavoidably, as when the mother dies giving birth. We are not wanting to judge or condemn our earthly mothers, who perhaps could not have done otherwise in difficult circumstances.

When praying for the healing of the difficult and painful memories, wounds and relationships of the past, it is normally a great help if we can to pray explicitly for the painful memories and relationships in question. So if fearful memories of a drunken father are involved, we should pray for the healing of those specific memories and for the relationship with the father. However we quite frequently do not know what it is that has damaged us, because the wounds and painful memories can be buried in our subconscious minds. Jesus can heal wounds which never do come up into the conscious mind. So it is good to pray for the healing of all the painful memories and wounds of the past, including those of which we are ignorant at the conscious level.

However, the Holy Spirit will sometimes give someone a 'word of knowledge' or a picture which can give us the clue to the cause of the wounds. Some people who are particularly gifted in this field may receive a very precise picture or 'word', such as a picture of a child with a brown dog if the death of a brown dog or the child being attacked by a brown dog is the difficult memory that needs to be healed. The age of the child at the time might also be given. I myself when praying for inner healing with a person sometimes find that a word like 'father' comes strongly into my mind, and this will influence the way I talk and pray with the person. Recently I was praying with a man for various things including inner healing when to my surprise the word 'beware' came strongly into my mind. This put me on my guard, and before long I realized that some of the things which the man was telling me about himself and his past were pure fabrications.

People are quite often mistaken as to which wound or relationship is the main cause of their difficulties. Recently three of us were praying with a very cultured and gifted middle-aged lady who was suffering from depression. She thought that the basic cause of the depression was the break-up of a relationship with a man whom she had hoped to marry. She also thought that memories in connection with her mother needed healing. However, when we started praying for the healing of the memories and relationships of the past, she collapsed in tears when our prayers were concerned with her father, who had been a cold and aloof man. It became apparent to us and to her that it was this relationship not the others which was the basic cause of her difficulties.

'From that time Jesus began to preach, saying, "Repent, for the kingdom of heaven is at hand" ' (Matthew 4:17). Jesus is still calling us all to repentance, and this can be the gateway leading to much inner healing. We have all reacted to the wounds and pressures of life imperfectly – often very imperfectly. Sin has entered into our reactions, sometimes at a very deep level, so that our emotional wounds have been affected and infected by sin. And repentance is the way to receive Jesus' healing and forgiveness from sin.

When we have been deeply wounded in life it is very easy just to blame other people, circumstances and even God for our pains and difficulties, while feeling very sorry for ourselves. This is very understandable – and very unhelpful! A great step forward has been taken when we realize that we need to repent and not just blame other people and circumstances. Sins like unforgiveness, anger, pride, lack of faith and hope – and others as well – inevitably play their part in our emotional wounds and problems. If we had perfect faith, hope and love, which of course no human being can have in this life, then we would not be afraid or anxious, because we would know that Jesus is in charge and that with him at our side there is nothing to fear: 'perfect love casts out fear' (1 John 4:18). So, without judging other people on account of their fears, we can repent of the lack of faith, hope and love present in our own anxieties and fears. We can also repent of the lack of faith and hope present in our false guilt. The Christian gospel teaches us that when we repent our sins are forgiven. Many Christians have truly repented of a sin but do not feel they have been forgiven, which shows lack of faith in Jesus' promise to forgive (cf. Luke 24:47).

We also need to repent of the way in which pride has influenced our emotional wounds. People can be depressed and feel suicidal because their worldly ambitions, status and reputation have collapsed. Not a little emotional sickness can be linked with wounded pride. To repent of our pride and to grow in humility can be very healing emotionally, and can transform painful memories of the past.

Forgiveness is the key to much or even most inner healing. The teaching of Jesus on forgiveness is very clear and very demanding. We are taught to pray: 'And forgive us our debts, as we also have forgiven our debtors' (Matthew 6:12). We are to forgive 'seventy times seven' (Matthew 18:22), which means we are to forgive indefinitely. And Jesus gave us the perfect example by forgiving those who put him to death: 'Father, forgive them; for they know not what they do' (Luke 23:34).

So often in practice our ideas on forgiveness are conditional: 'I would forgive him if he apologized'; 'I would have forgiven her if she had not done it deliberately'; 'I would forgive him if he had not done it so many times'; 'I would forgive her if she were not continuing to do it'; 'I would have forgiven him if it were myself and not my child who had been attacked'; 'I would forgive if the offence had not been so deliberately cruel and malicious'; 'I would forgive her if she had not ruined my whole life'. But the teaching of Jesus is clear and simple: we are called to forgive everything always, without any exceptions. Whenever we have failed to forgive fully we need to repent and ask for the grace to do so. We are also told: 'Love your enemies and pray for those who persecute you' (Matthew 5:44). The test as to how far we have really forgiven those who have hurt us is often how truly we are loving and praying for them.

Often people are aware that they have not forgiven or fully forgiven someone or some group of people. I once asked a priest who came to me for ministry if he had fully forgiven everyone. He replied immediately: 'No, I have not forgiven my father.' Well, we knew where we were, which was an advantage. However, often people are not aware that they have not forgiven someone or some group, as was my position before I 'rested in the Spirit' when Francis MacNutt prayed for me, as I mentioned in the last chapter. So when someone answers my question about forgiveness by saying immediately: 'No, Father, I have forgiven everyone everything', I know that there may be quite a lot of hidden unforgiveness under the surface. For example, a Polish exile may not have fully forgiven the Russians or the Communists or the Germans or the Nazis for his own past sufferings and those of his family, or a person of one race may not have fully forgiven people of another race. Or someone may not have fully forgiven their father or mother, but this may have been suppressed in the subconscious mind, because the idea of not loving and forgiving them is unacceptable, something too difficult to face.

I remember a man telling me that he had only just learned to forgive his mother for dying when he was three. What did he mean, for his mother had not committed suicide or anything like that? He knew with his rational mind that there was nothing to forgive. But deep down in him there had remained a little boy of three who was furious with his mother for disappearing when she was greatly needed. Hidden within many of us there are still angry children who have not fully forgiven.

Forgiveness is fundamentally an act of the will, so we can basically forgive even when we are feeling very angry at the level of the emotions. However perfect forgiveness involves the emotions also, and we must often pray that our forgiveness will flow from the will into the emotions and into the subconscious mind.

I know a deeply spiritual priest who says that he tries to forgive an offence within ten seconds – while many of us are still floundering around ten minutes, ten hours, ten days, ten weeks, ten months, or ten years later! It is a great grace to learn to forgive quickly. When we do not forgive we are the first victims of our unforgiveness, for we cannot experience the peace, joy, love and healing which Jesus wants to give us if we are not at least trying to forgive.

We are called to forgive in three directions: other people, God and ourselves. Of course we know that objectively there is never anything to forgive our infinitely loving God. But we can be very angry with God for having allowed this or that to happen in our lives: the break-up of a marriage, the death of a child, financial disasters, the collapse of our health. So we have to repent of all bitterness and resentment over the hard knocks we have received in life.

Many people cannot forgive themselves for their past sins (e.g. an abortion), for their past mistakes, for having made a mess of their lives. Well, we have all sinned, we have all made mistakes, we have all made a mess of our lives in one way or another. The good news of the gospel is that Jesus came to save and heal sinners, not 'good people' – the greatest saint is basically a saved sinner! We are to love our neighbour as *ourselves*, and this involves learning to forgive ourselves. If Jesus can forgive us when we repent, then we can also forgive ourselves.

Unforgiveness, bitterness, resentment and wrong anger are not only spiritual and emotional sicknesses, they can also affect our physical health. The statistics show us that during the eighteen months after the death or departure of a spouse, when there can be much unforgiveness, bitterness, resentment and anger, people are considerably more likely to get cancer than at other times. And there have been cases of cancer disappearing when people learned to forgive. Frequently we find that there can be a link between arthritis and unforgiveness, bitterness, resentment and wrong anger. So forgiveness can also often be the key to physical healing. On many occasions when I am asked to pray for physical healing I ask the person whether they have forgiven everyone everything, for this may be the root of the trouble.

Now I must make an important point. When we encourage people to repent of lack of faith and hope, of unforgiveness, bitterness, resentment, wrong anger, pride and other sins, we must make it very clear that we are not judging them or condemning them. For so many of the people who come to us for inner healing, it is much more a case of having been sinned against than of sinning. We must not burden them with false guilt. What we can say to them is that we have all sinned, that we are all called to grow in repentance, and that repentance is very healing and liberating for all of us. It may well be that the parent, or husband, or whoever has caused the wound may need to repent one hundred times more. But our job is to repent for our own sins, not for those of others!

One last point in this chapter: it is right to pray for and seek prayers for our inner healing. And since it is normally a gradual process, it is right to continue to pray for it. However, we must avoid an exaggerated concentration on ourselves and our problems, including our need for inner healing. Too much praying for our inner healing can be a sign of being too self-centred. Having prayed we need to get on with praising God and helping other people. Indeed, sometimes the very act of forgetting ourselves, concentrating on praising God and helping other people can be the royal road towards inner healing!

8

Praying For Deliverance

And he called the twelve together and gave them power and authority over all demons and to cure diseases, and he sent them out to preach the kingdom of God and to heal. (Luke 9:1–2)

The seventy returned with joy, saying: 'Lord, even the demons are subject to us in your name!' And he said to them, 'I saw Satan fall like lightning from heaven. Behold, I have given you authority to tread upon serpents and scorpions, and over all the power of the enemy; and nothing shall hurt you.' (Luke 10:17–19)

And these signs will accompany those who believe: in my name they will cast out demons. (Mark 16:17)

From these and other texts in the New Testament it would seem clear that the devil and other demons exist and that at any rate some disciples of Jesus are called to cast them out. I find it strange therefore to meet Christians, including some Catholics, who do not believe in a personal devil or personal demons and who therefore do not believe in casting them out. Perhaps in this field some Catholics have been over-influenced in the ecumenical dialogue by liberal Protestants and insufficiently influenced by evangelical Protestants, by the Pentecostals and by the Eastern Orthodox. In his general audience on 15 November 1972, Pope Paul VI asked the question: 'What are the greatest needs of the Church today?' This is how he replied:

Do not let our answer surprise you as being oversimple or even superstitious and unreal: one of the greatest needs is defence from that evil which is called the Devil. Evil is not merely a lack of something, but an effective agent, a living, spiritual being, perverted and perverting. A terrible reality. It is contrary to the teaching of the Bible and the Church to refuse to recognize the existence of such a reality . . . or to explain it as a pseudo reality, a conceptual and fanciful personification of the unknown causes of our misfortunes. That it is not a question of one devil, but of many, is indicated by the various passages in the Gospel (Luke 11:21; Mark 5:9). But the principal one is Satan, which means the adversary, the enemy; and with him, many, creatures of God, but fallen, because of their rebellion and damnation – a whole mysterious world, upset by the unhappy drama, of which we know very little.

(L'Osservatore Romano, 23 November 1972)

Pope John Paul II, in his general audience on the 13 August 1986, makes it very clear that the official teaching of the Catholic Church includes the belief in the existence of both a personal devil, Satan, and of other personal demons. Towards the end of this talk, the Pope said:

To conclude, we must add that the impressive words of the Apostle John, 'The whole world lies under the power of the evil one' (1 John 5:19), allude also to the presence of Satan in the history of humanity, a presence which becomes all the more acute when man and society depart from God. The influence of the evil spirit can conceal itself in a more profound and effective way: it is in his 'interests' to make himself unknown. Satan has the skill to deny his existence in the name of rationalism and of every other system of thought which seeks all possible means to avoid recognizing his activity. This, however, does not signify the elimination of man's free will and responsibility, and even less the frustration of the saving action of Christ. It is, rather, a case of a conflict between the dark powers of evil and the power of redemption.

According to the Code of Canon Law (Canon 1172), 'No one may lawfully exorcize the possessed without the special and express permission of the local Ordinary. This permission is to be granted by the local Ordinary only to a priest who is endowed with piety, knowledge, prudence and integrity of life.' So in the Catholic Church solemn exorcism may only be carried out by a priest specially appointed by the local bishop.

In this chapter I am not writing about solemn exorcism of the possessed, which would in any case be beyond the scope of my competence. However, the need for deliverance from demonic possession is relatively rare, while deliverance from various degrees of demonic oppression is very much commoner. To understand the whole question of trouble from the devil perhaps I can make a comparison with physical illness. We can say that someone is suffering from sickness, and that can be anything from the beginning of a sore throat to the last stages of terminal cancer. So it is with trouble from the devil or 'demonisation'. John Richards sees it as a long thin wedge. At the thin end of the wedge there are the 'flaming darts of the evil one' (Ephesians 6:16) by which we are all attacked frequently – it may be a stronger than normal temptation or feeling of fear or depression (the 'flaming dart' is often directed at and adds to an existing spiritual or psychological weakness). At the thick edge of the wedge there are things like demonic possession and deep involvement in Satanism.

When someone says to me that they think they are being attacked by the devil and need deliverance ministry, I quite often reply that we are all being frequently attacked by the devil, that we all need deliverance from these attacks, and that every time we say the Our Father we are praying for deliverance: 'But deliver us from evil' – which certainly includes deliverance from evil spirits.

The important question is not whether we are being attacked by the devil or other evil spirits, which we all often are, as we can see when reading the lives and spiritual writings of many saints, but how seriously and in what ways we are being attacked. Some people are very frightened at the idea that they may be being attacked by the devil and need deliverance ministry. It can help to take away this fear if we explain to them that we are all involved in spiritual warfare, that 'fiery darts' are shot at all of us, that this is a normal experience in the Christian life. St Paul is saying to us all: 'Put on the whole armour of God, that you may be able to stand against the wiles of the devil. For we are not contending against flesh and blood, but against the principalities, against the powers, against the world rulers of this present darkness, against the spiritual hosts of wickedness in the heavenly places' (Ephesians 6:11–13) (cf. also 1 Peter 5:8–11).

We can often be delivered from less serious attacks of the devil and lesser degrees of demonisation by the normal practices of the life of prayer, such as going to confession or receiving Jesus in communion, or participating in a prayer meeting. Frequently someone will go to Mass feeling spiritually oppressed and burdened, and after Mass they will be at peace and spiritually refreshed. In many such cases there has, I think, been some deliverance from evil spirits. Again, it has been the experience of many of us that intense praise at a prayer meeting has liberated us from feelings of spiritual heaviness or agitation – and I am convinced that frequently this has involved deliverance from evil spirits, who obviously would not feel at home in an atmosphere of authentic praise.

Indeed the ways to receive deliverance from evil spirits and to receive inner healing are often largely the same. In both cases repentance, forgiveness, praise and the use of the sacraments can play a key part. This is not surprising, for there is much overlapping between psychological and emotional sickness on the one hand and demonic attacks and bondages on the other. A sickness which is basically psychological or emotional can be aggravated by the fiery darts of the devil; and a problem which is largely demonic will have its psychological and emotional repercussions. So in practice I think we often have to be aware that we are dealing with a problem which involves both inner healing and deliverance from the attacks of evil spirits.

When possible it is good to deal with demonisation by praying for inner healing and for the infilling of the Holy Spirit. I remember Abbot David M. Geraets OSB of Pecos in New Mexico (USA) saying that many cases can better be dealt with by praying for inner healing. They could be dealt with by casting out demons but there is less danger of problems arising if the inner healing approach is adopted. The Pecos monastic community has seen very remarkable healings from even very serious cases of demonisation by the inner healing and infilling approach.

Perhaps this is the right place to say that I agree with those people who think that 'fiery darts of the evil one' can sometimes affect our physical health, as was the case of the 'woman who had had a spirit of infirmity for eighteen years' and concerning whom Jesus said: 'And ought not this woman, a daughter of Abraham whom Satan bound for eighteen years, be loosened from this bond on the sabbath day?' (Luke 13:10–17). I believe the devil will sometimes try to stop people doing the work God wants them to do by attacking their physical health – I think that this has happened to me at times. 'Fiery darts of the evil one' can sometimes aggravate an existing physical weakness or sickness, or even perhaps cause a physical illness. So I believe that there is sometimes a place for rebuking an evil spirit of infirmity troubling oneself or another person. However, it is important to add that all sickness is not of course directly the work of the devil.

Not all cases of demonisation seem to respond to the inner healing and infilling approach, and this appears to be especially true of the more serious cases. In England and probably in many other countries also, involvement in things like Satanism, Voodoo, Witchcraft, Spiritualism, violence and perverted sexual activity seem to be on the increase, and this is surely causing a growing number of heavily demonised people. Here we need to remember that Jesus has given to his Church a ministry of casting out devils, a ministry which, I think, is very much neglected by Catholics in many places.

What is happening in some areas is that more and more

Catholics are going to members of other churches in order to receive deliverance ministry. I personally know of Anglican clergy who are gifted and have experience in this ministry to whom a considerable number of Catholics go. I heard of a case in the USA where a Catholic layman was seeking deliverance ministry. The diocesan authorities dithered and delayed over the matter for six months, with the result that the man in question lost patience and went one evening to the local Pentecostal church down the road, where he received effective deliverance ministry within half an hour!

I consider a big part of our problem is that the Catholic clergy in general have received no training in this field and have no experience in it – whereas every Pentecostal pastor would have received practical training in the deliverance ministry. When studying for the priesthood I listened to learned lectures for many hours on the heresies of the first few centuries in the Church, but no one gave me any instruction on how I might recognize whether or not a person was in need of serious deliverance ministry.

There is a further problem for Catholics. If it is judged that the demonised person may be possessed, then this case will be referred to the diocesan exorcist – if there is one – who will minister to the person probably after they have been examined by a psychiatrist. But all this takes quite a lot of time to arrange, and some demonised people may need urgent attention. I know of a case in which an Anglican priest experienced in this ministry was asked to minister to someone in another diocese. The Anglican bishop of the diocese insisted that the person in question should see a psychiatrist first – and the man committed suicide before this could be arranged! Suicidal or violent cases may need immediate attention.

Catholic bishops and priests are understandably and indeed rightly cautious when it comes to serious cases of demonisation. In the ministry of casting out demons things can go wrong, and indeed very wrong. A few years ago in the London borough in which I live a wandering evangelical preacher and his friend attempted to exorcize a woman at her request. In trying to get the demons out of her they stamped on her body – and this killed her. They then prayed for twelve hours for her resurrection, which needless to say did not happen. They then handed themselves over to the police. So it is obviously important not to let just anyone and everyone loose on the ministry of casting out demons.

However cautiousness by itself is not enough. If we only play safe, which I suspect is what many of us Catholic priests are doing, then seriously demonised people who are in desperate need of help are not going to receive it, at least not from the Catholic Church. Doubtless many Catholics have been wonderfully helped through deliverance ministry from members of other churches. Some Catholics however have not found this ministry helpful. And there is a danger that Catholics who go to other Christians for this ministry may imbibe along with it teaching which is not in accord with the doctrine of the Catholic Church. I am worried when Catholics, sometimes influenced by *some* non-Catholic literature or preaching, seem to have developed 'demonitis', the seeing of demons where there are none, the blaming of all our troubles on demons, endless talk about demons. (Our minds need to be fixed on God, on Jesus. Too much thinking and talking about demons are to be avoided.)

All this underlines, in my opinion, the need for the Catholic Church to wake up to the problems of serious demonisation in our society. In his book, *Renewal and the Powers of Darkness* (Darton, Longman and Todd, 1983), Cardinal Suenens has a heading, 'The necessity of a new pastoral teaching on the subject of exorcism' (page 96). Surely there is such a necessity, for some Catholics, including a few priests, do not even believe in the existence of the devil and a few other Catholics have caught 'demonitis'. Of the two problems, I believe the failure to face up to the needs of seriously demonised people is much bigger and more widespread than the excesses of 'demonitis', serious though the latter can be.

In his book Cardinal Suenens raises an interesting possibility:

I would add that if the office of exorcist has disappeared as a minor order, there is nothing to prevent an episcopal conference from requesting Rome to restore it. I do not know if this is advisable, but it is at least a possibility which is deserving of study. If the conclusion is positive, then the office of exorcist could be made available to qualified laymen. (page 97)

We need to recognize that some people have special gifts in the area of exorcism – and I do not consider myself to be one of them – that laymen and women are sometimes gifted in this way (not only the clergy), and that authentic gifts of this kind should not be wasted, especially at a time when the needs are so great.

Teaching people how to cast out demons goes beyond the scope of this book, which is concerned with praying for healing in general. Apart from the fact that there are other people more qualified than I am to write on the ministry of exorcism, I would be somewhat fearful of indiscriminately encouraging people to go round trying to cast out demons, which could lead to many casualties. On the subject of casting out, may I recommend the excellent booklet by James McManus CSSR, *The Ministry of Deliverance in the Catholic Tradition*, obtainable from the National Service Committee for Catholic Charismatic Renewal, 424 Kings Road, London SW10 0LF. In this booklet the author goes through the five stages of the prayer of praise, the prayer for protection, the prayer of binding, the prayer of casting out and the prayer for the infilling of the Holy Spirit (page 26). He also makes the valuable point that 'the prayer for deliverance is ordinarily made in silence' (page 30), which can help to avoid all sorts of problems.

Could I now make two strong pleas, the first to the authorities in the Catholic Church? Could the bishops remind Catholics of the teaching of the Catholic Church which forbids us to get involved in the occult, for such involvement can lead to varying degrees of demonisation? The occult includes such obvious things as Satanism, Voodoo, Witchcraft (black and white), but also Spiritualism and all attempts to divine the future. So ouija boards, astrology, tarot cards, palm reading, crystal gazing and similar things are out for the Christian (see Deuteronomy 18:9–14). Those of us involved in the healing ministry know how many Catholics do in fact go to spiritualists for healing and how many see no wrong in astrology or palm reading. We also know how many pupils in Catholic schools are playing with ouija boards and tarot cards.

My second plea is to those Christians who are aware of the dangers of involvement in the occult. Please do not exaggerate the limits of the occult, for this leads to classifying as demonic things which are not, and causes some other Christians to regard all warnings about the dangers of the occult as ridiculous. There are some Christians who are saying that all osteopathy, homoeopathy, hypnotism, acupuncture, ju-jitsu, yoga, water divining, pyschoanalysis and extra sensory perception are occult and therefore demonic. Doubtless, in varying degrees, there can be dangers in some of the practices listed above, and people may sometimes need to be warned of the dangers. But that is no excuse for simply describing them all as demonic! Otherwise a good Christian whom God has healed through the hands of an osteopath will simply think we are fanatics.

May I make a special appeal here to Catholics involved in the Charismatic Renewal. The fact that a Pentecostal or Evangelical Christian is a very devout disciple of Jesus, has a wonderful healing ministry and is a great evangelist, does not mean that we should accept his teaching all along the line. Let us thank God for his gifts and for what he does for the building up of God's Kingdom, but let us remember where his beliefs would differ from our own. This is relevant for the subject under discussion above. Many Pentecostals and Evangelicals simply regard all non-Christian religions and things linked with them as demonic. The Second Vatican Council in its 'Declaration on the Relationship of the Church to Non-Christian Religions' states that:

The Catholic Church rejects nothing which is true and holy in these religions. She looks with sincere respect upon those ways of conduct and of life, those rules and teachings which, though differing in many particulars from what she holds and sets forth, nevertheless often reflect a ray of that Truth which enlightens all men. Indeed, she proclaims and must ever proclaim Christ, 'the way, the truth and the life' (John 14:6), in whom men find the fulness of religious life, and in whom God has reconciled all things to Himself (cf. 2 Corinthians 5:18–19).

So we Catholics must not be surprised if we find that we do not always agree with Pentecostals and Evangelicals on the subject of the limits of the occult and the demonic, just as we do not agree with them on the rightness of asking Our Lady to pray for us. If Catholics involved in the Charismatic Renewal adopt a Pentecostal rather than a Catholic position on certain subjects, this will put other Catholics off the Charismatic Renewal, which they will regard as not being truly Catholic. I think that it is a great pity when this happens, for I am convinced that the Charismatic Renewal has much to give to the Catholic Church.

On the whole question of the Catholic attitude towards non-Christian religions and towards various forms of unconventional healing and alternative medicine, may I very strongly recommend three excellent articles by Fr Michael Simpson sj in *Good News*, numbers 76, 77 and 78, 1988 (obtainable from The National Service Committee for Catholic Charismatic Renewal, 484 Kings Road, London SW10 0LF). Having pointed out various very real dangers in this field, Father Michael ends his last, wise and well-balanced article by saying: 'We must not dismiss as demonic or dangerous what, if practised with wisdom and in a way centred on Christ, may in truth be part of God's creative plan for our growth to wholeness in body, mind and spirit.'

At the end of this chapter there is one more thing which needs to be said. Although the devil and demons may sometimes give us a difficult time – as they did to Jesus during his temptation in the wilderness – if we are truly trying to follow Jesus and to trust in him, then we have nothing to fear from the powers of darkness. We read in the Letter of St James (4:7): 'Submit yourselves therefore to God. Resist the devil and he will flee from you.' And St Paul writes: 'I would have you wise as to what is good and guileless as to what is evil; then the God of peace will soon crush Satan under your feet' (Romans 16:19). So in truth Satan and the demons have more to fear from us than we have from them, if we keep our eyes fixed on Jesus and if his praises are on our lips and in our hearts. Alleluia!

9

Gifts of Healing and Healing Teams

All Christians are called to pray for healing. All Catholics pray for healing when they participate in the prayers of the Mass which ask for healing, including physical healing – see Chapter 3 on 'Praying for healing and the sacraments'. Jesus is saying to all Christians: 'Ask, and it will be given you; seek, and you will find; knock, and it will be opened to you' (Luke 11:9). All authentic prayer is answered and makes a difference, even if it is not in the way we first hoped. Praying for the healing of spirits, minds and bodies should be a normal part of the prayer life of every Christian.

However, some Christians, according to St Paul, have gifts of healing: 'To each is given the manifestation of the Spirit for the common good. To one is given through the Spirit the utterance of wisdom . . . to another gifts of healing by the one Spirit' (1 Corinthians 12:7) – the Greek text actually speaks of 'gifts of healings'. There are also two further references to this gift at the end of chapter 12 of 1 Corinthians. So while all Christians should pray for healing and God will use their prayers to heal, some have special gifts and special ministries in this field and are used more often and more powerfully than others to heal through prayer.

St Paul's teaching on this subject is confirmed by experience in our prayer groups. We find that just as some members of the prayer groups have gifts of teaching, others have gifts for the music ministry, and others are gifted in administration, so some members of our prayer groups are gifted in the healing ministry. (Of course, people often have more than one gift.)

If people would look upon the gift of healing in the same

way that they do other gifts of the Spirit like teaching and administration, then many of the difficulties regarding the ministry of healing would disappear. A main source of difficulty is the tendency among many Catholics to link gifts of healing with sanctity in a way they would not, for example, link the gifts of teaching and administration with it. So if someone exercises a special ministry of healing, he must be a saint or be claiming to be a saint. There is nothing in the New Testament to suggest that one needs to be more of a saint to exercise the gift of healing than to use gifts of teaching or administration. The exercise of all the gifts of the Spirit will in fact go wrong if we are not seeking sanctity. But God does not wait for Christians to be saints before he uses them to teach or administer – and the same applies to healing. There are holy priests who do not have gifts of teaching and preaching, and there are less holy priests who do have these gifts. In the same way, there are holy Christians who do not have a gift of healing, and less holy Christians who do. However, our gifts will flourish more as through the grace of God we grow in holiness – or become less unholy! And the exercise of every ministry, healing like the others, should be a stimulant to seek to grow in holiness. So let us try to apply the same Christian common sense to healing that we apply to the other gifts of the Spirit.

Since 1972 I must have met well over a hundred Catholics who have received and are exercising gifts of healing – and I have also met many Christians in other churches of whom this is true. Most of these Christians have certainly not got very powerful gifts of healing – but usually they are growing gifts. The great majority of these Christians came into the healing ministry through involvement in the Charismatic Renewal, where there is a greater awareness and encouragement of the gift of healing. However, I also know Christians whose reception of the gift of healing was not via the Charismatic Renewal – I think of a Catholic lady who was the headmistress of a school. She was made an extraordinary minister of communion, and she found that when she prayed for sick people to whom she was giving communion, healings started to happen. She has now retired early from being headmistress and has started a house of prayer, where she exercises a powerful ministry of healing.

Perhaps an analogy will help here, an analogy between praying for healing and singing. Everyone – or nearly everyone – can sing, and every Christian can pray for healing. Some people have special gifts of singing, and some Christians have special gifts of praying for healing. Some people have outstanding gifts of singing, and some Christians have outstandingly powerful gifts or ministries of healing, like Monsignor Michael Buckley and Ian Andrews in England.

In general we should, I think, do far more to encourage all Christians to pray for healing, including physical healing. There are in our churches some Christians who simply do not believe in praying for healing, at least physical healing; there are other Christians who do not pray for healing because they think that their own prayers are not powerful enough to make any difference; and there are others who do not pray for healing because they think that they are not worthy to do so, that they are too big a sinner to ask God for anybody's healing. All these Christians need to understand that people are healed in answer to prayer not because we are worthy but because Jesus is worthy, not because our prayers are powerful but because Jesus' love is powerful. John Wimber is surely right in encouraging all Christians to step out in faith and pray for healing.

Only two days ago I witnessed the surprise and joy of a Catholic extraordinary minister of communion who a few days earlier had visited a woman in hospital suffering much from spinal trouble. She was depressed and had said 'No' to the offer of Holy Communion, but she allowed the extraordinary minister of communion to say a prayer over her for healing, a practice to which he was new. When he returned to the ward a few days later he was very surprised to see the woman with a big smile on her face and lying very much more comfortably in her bed. She told him that a few hours after his previous visit she was suddenly filled with peace, and then she found that her back was much better. This time the woman accepted

Holy Communion. I think that Jesus wants this sort of thing to happen far more often and through the prayers of far more Christians. So I would, in general, encourage Christians to step out in faith and pray for healing in a simple way, especially within their family and among friends.

Not every Christian however is called to a special ministry of healing, not every Christian is called to join the healing team of the prayer group or of the parish. The analogy with singing may help again. All Christians should be encouraged to sing in church, but not all are called to join the church choir. We have to recognize that the presence of some people on a healing team will not be helpful, indeed will be harmful. There can be several reasons for this: they may lack discretion and discernment; they may be too much in need of healing themselves; they may be too mentally or emotionally disturbed; they may, so to speak, pass on 'negative vibes' if they lay hands on people; or they may simply not be gifted in praying for healing.

The leaders of a prayer group, or healing team, or the clergy have both the duty of encouraging suitable people to join the healing team and of preventing unsuitable individuals from becoming involved. I find that in practice this is the most difficult side of leadership of a healing team – just as it can be to decide who should join the parish catechetical team or finance committee. I think that normally a leadership team needs to meet and pray together to try to discern God's will concerning membership of a healing team; I believe that it is normally better to have collective rather than individual discernment, and a collective decision makes it all less personal.

Inevitably there will be times when we have to say 'No' to someone who asks to join the healing team, and unavoidably people will sometimes be very hurt by this – just as people are very disappointed sometimes when they are not accepted for the parish catechetical team or finance committee.

We have to accept the important principles that no one is the final discerner of their own gifts, and that everyone needs to exercise their gifts under submission. We may be convinced that God is calling us to this or that ministry and it may be right to inform the leadership of the prayer group or the parish clergy of our conviction. However, we have to accept their decision in this and similar matters. Eventually, of course, final discernment is with the bishop for the diocese.

Decisions concerning the membership of healing teams and the healing ministry in general are obviously not infallible, and inevitably human factors such as ignorance, prejudice, fear, pride, or even jealousy will sometimes play their part. However, we have to accept the decisions of the competent authority. The alternative to this is chaos, in which people claiming to have hot lines to God go round doing their own thing and causing harm – and bringing the healing ministry into disrepute. We must believe that Jesus is Lord of the situation, and that even when a mistaken decision has been made, God will bring good out of evil if we let him. For instance, it may be that if someone is mistakenly not accepted onto the healing team of one prayer group, God will arrange for them to minister in another prayer group. We must trust that if God has given someone a gift and wants them to use it, then he will open a door to make that possible. However, in my experience, healing teams do not often make mistakes about membership.

Every ministry, whether it be teaching, administration, or healing, can start going off the rails. Ministering under submission provides a necessary check. It can be a wonderful blessing for the person with a gift of healing   and especially for someone with a great gift – in protecting them from, amongst other things, too many demands on their ministry, which can lead to 'burn-out'. Everyone in the healing ministry has to learn to say 'No' at times to requests for ministry, otherwise they may well crack up from exhaustion. It can make it much easier to say 'No' when it is done out of obedience to someone with some kind of authority – the leader of a healing team, a parish priest, a religious superior, or a spiritual guide. I sometimes think that if the devil cannot stop someone getting involved in the healing ministry he will often try to drown them in it!

Belonging to a healing team has many advantages over being a loner. Members of a healing team can encourage each other, support each other, pray for each other's ministries, and pray for healing for each other. I personally have been wonderfully supported and helped both in myself and in my ministry by other members of our healing teams in the last fifteen years or so – and I know of many other people who would say the same thing.

It is good for members of a healing team to meet together regularly on their own for prayer, sharing, teaching, discussion and for ministry. The members of a London prayer group healing team have been meeting together for a day every few months for years now, and this has been a source of real blessing. The getting in sometimes of an outside speaker on these occasions has helped us to widen our horizons and take stock of our ministry.

When actually praying with sick or needy people there are advantages in praying in twos or threes or even sometimes in larger groups if this is possible. The discernment, prayers and gifts of a group are usually more powerful than those of a single individual. A complementarity of gifts and experience can come into play. One member of a team may be more gifted in praying for physical healing, another member for inner healing. I often prefer to leave a married person to lead the praying over people with marriage problems, since they will probably understand the situation better than I do. And there are obviously times when it is more suitable for a man to minister to a man and a woman to a woman.

At times we have to minister on our own because no one else is available or for reasons of discretion – often I pray alone with a person after hearing their confession. However, sometimes it is better to delay or postpone the ministry until someone else can join us in it. I myself will sometimes refuse to pray other than very briefly over a disturbed woman unless another woman member of our healing team can be present to minister with me.

May I now make a plea to Christians involved in the healing ministry? Please be careful about criticizing each other's ministries. Obviously there are times when we have to be critical, when we may have to say that we think someone's healing ministry is lacking in one direction or another, or needs to be looked into, or even that we think someone should stop ministering. But all too easily too human motives can enter into our criticism. After all, we are sinners like other people and we suffer from pride, ambition, envy, jealousy and self-seeking like everybody else – our motives for being in the healing ministry are never one hundred per cent perfect. I have had to fight feelings of envy and jealousy in myself in connection with the healing ministry. We need to recognize the less worthy motives which may be influencing us. Indeed, I would be worried about someone in the healing ministry who thought that their motives for being involved in it were entirely perfect – that would merely show that they did not truly know themselves. It is easier to deal with our weaknesses if we recognize them.

For a number of years now I have been recommending to members of healing ministry teams that they should pray daily for the gift of humility in connection with the healing ministry. Greater humility would lead to greater unity and harmony in the healing ministry. It would also allow God to give us greater gifts of healing, for the more humble we are the more we will give the glory to God. (I think God may sometimes be saying to himself: 'I would like to give Benedict greater gifts of healing, but I cannot do so at present because his head would burst with pride!') We have to recognize that 'successes' in the healing ministry can be heady stuff for us poor sinners. I remember the case of a woman who came with her husband from a distance to me for prayer for depression. After the prayer she insisted on kissing my hands fervently, saying that: 'These have been the hands of Jesus Christ for me tonight.' I never heard from her again. Perhaps a week later she was saying that the visit to Dom Benedict had been a complete waste of time: we need to take the praise with a pinch of salt – and in any case give the glory to God!

Perhaps a 'code of humility' could be drawn up for those of us in the healing ministry:

(1) Be willing to accept the discernment and guidance of other suitable people concerning your healing ministry.

(2) Other things being equal, let the other person lead the healing prayer and be in the limelight.

(3) Remember and talk about not only your 'successes' but also your 'failures' in the healing ministry.

(4) Talk not only about your 'successes' but also about the 'successes' of others in the healing ministry – indeed, preferably talk about the 'successes' of others.

(5) Seek not only to exercise the healing ministry but also to spread it.

(6) It can be good to pray that the Holy Spirit will empower you more strongly in the healing ministry – but do not only pray this prayer for yourself.

(7) Rejoice at the 'successes' of others and when others are more gifted than yourself in the healing ministry.

If I have stressed the importance of humility in the healing ministry, my intention is in no way to discourage suitable people from entering it, but rather to safeguard it. As I shall explain in the next chapter, I believe God wants more and more suitable people to enter the healing ministry. And if this ministry can be a tiring one, it can also be a very rewarding one, bringing with it true joy. As we seek in humility to be authentic channels of Jesus' healing love – for, of course, it is not we who heal – we shall find that we ourselves are increasingly healed, are increasingly made whole.

The Healing Challenge
and Evangelism

Praying for healing miracles is part of the historical tradition of the Catholic Church and of the Eastern Orthodox and other Eastern churches. There never has been a time when members of these churches were not praying for healing miracles and when people were not being healed in answer to prayer. Doubtless the ministry of praying for healing has flourished more at certain periods of the Church's history than at others, and in some places more than in others. But praying for healing miracles has been a constant strand in the life of the Catholic and Eastern churches.

The tradition of the Protestant Reformation has been otherwise. Its two main founding fathers, Martin Luther (c. 1483–1546) and John Calvin (c. 1509–64), basically accepted the doctrine called Dispensationalism, which regarded healing miracles and the exercise of the gift of healing as being only intended for the first generation of Christians. However, in the history of Protestantism there have been people like George Fox (c. 1624–91), the founder of the Quakers, and John Wesley (c. 1703–91), the father of Methodism, who went directly to the New Testament in their attitude to healing and who were used to perform healing miracles.

Given the unbroken Catholic tradition of praying for healing miracles and the absence of that tradition in so much Protestant history, it is ecumenically paradoxical that today there is often in practice more openness to praying for healing miracles in churches descended from or connected with the Protestant Reformation than in the Catholic Church. In England today there is more praying for healing, especially physical healing, in the Pentecostal and charismatic churches than in most Catholic parishes. And the Anglican Communion often also seems to be ahead of us in this field. The Lambeth Conferences of Anglican bishops have been considering positively the healing ministry of prayer since as far back as 1908. In 1958 a commission set up by the Archbishops of Canterbury and York produced a lengthy and remarkable report 'The Church's Ministry of Healing', which was approved by the Lambeth Conference of that year, and which did much to encourage and guide the healing ministry of prayer. The 1978 Lambeth Conference affirmed:

(1) 'that the healing of the sick in his Name is as much part of the proclamation of the Kingdom as the preaching of the good news of Jesus Christ'
(2) 'that to neglect this aspect of ministry is to diminish our part in Christ's total redemptive activity'.

Furthermore, the seriousness with which the Church of England is taking the healing ministry of prayer is shown by the fact that an Anglican bishop personally involved full-time in the healing ministry, Morris Maddocks, has been appointed 'Adviser for the Ministry of Health and Healing to the Archbishops of Canterbury and York'.

May I express the hope that soon the healing ministry of prayer is going to be taken equally seriously and positively at the official level in the Catholic Church? And also that we are going to see before long an official Catholic statement as serious as the eighty-five page 1958 Lambeth Conference report? In October 1985 Rome did in fact publish a report on 'Sects or New Religious Movements: Pastoral Challenge', produced by the Vatican Secretariat for Promoting Christian Unity, the Secretariat for Non-Christians, the Secretariat for Non-Believers and the Pontifical Council for Culture, in which we read: 'Special attention should be paid to the experiential dimension, i.e. discovering Christ personally through prayer and dedication (e.g. charismatic and "born again" movements). Many Christians live as if they had never been born at all! Special attention must be given to the healing ministry through prayers, reconciliation, fellowship and care' (section 3, paragraph 3. See the English edition of the Osservatore Romano, 19 May 1986, page 6). May this brief encouraging reference to the healing ministry of prayer be followed by fuller statements before long.

In quite a few countries an increasing number of Catholics seem to be going elsewhere in search of healing through prayer and other spiritual means – and they are seeking elsewhere among non-Catholics because they are not in practice being offered much in the way of prayer for healing in their Catholic parishes. If one goes to a public healing service run by a Pentecostal evangelist like Steve Ryder, one will find a considerable number of Catholics there seeking healing. In an ecumenical age this is not surprising. The healing ministry of prayer crosses the frontiers between the churches and can make a real contribution to the cause of Christian unity. When God uses a Protestant to heal a Catholic and a Catholic to heal a Protestant, then some healing has also taken place in the divisions between the churches. Indeed, I think we should encourage ecumenical healing services. But can a Catholic feel entirely happy that it is much more often a question of Catholics seeking healing from Evangelicals and Pentecostals, and not often the other way round – although I know a Methodist who on one of our pilgrimages to Lourdes received remarkable physical healings?

The relative absence of opportunities of being prayed with for healing in Catholic parishes is leading to something really dangerous in another direction. Far more Catholics than commonly realized are going to spiritualists and non-Christian healers in search of healing, sometimes with disastrous results. I know of the case of a Catholic man who went to an Eastern guru in London for healing. The Catholic man paid a large sum of money for an object of Eastern piety which, it was said, would help his healing, and after this he felt he was caught up in some spiritual bondage. I think of the Catholic woman who suffered much from her back and went to spiritualists for healing. She stopped practising as a Catholic, became deeply involved in Spiritualism, and by the time she came to see me ten years later, her main problems had become mental instability and strong suicidal tendencies – the back was still bad. And in case anyone should think it is only fringe Catholics who go to spiritualist and similar healers, I will mention the lady who was a pillar of the catechetical work in her parish, and who on becoming seriously ill went several times to a spiritualist healer, under pressure from a kind neighbour.

All these Catholics went elsewhere seeking healing because they did not think they could find it in the Catholic Church. Here is a challenge. We are living at a time when non-Christian faith healing is increasing and receiving more and more publicity and attention. If we do not renew the healing ministry of prayer in the Catholic Church, in fidelity to the New Testament and to the tradition of the Catholic Church, then certainly more and more Catholics will go elsewhere seeking healing, sometimes with disastrous consequences.

Being aware of and renewing the healing dimension of the sacraments is probably not going to cause difficulties for the majority of Catholics – indeed, I think most will welcome it with joy (see Chapter 3). Doubtless the sacramental side of the healing ministry is a special contribution which the Catholic Church can make to the ecumenical dialogue on the healing ministry. Here I think the Evangelicals and Pentecostals have something important to learn from us. It was, I think, significant that when an evangelical lady was reading the earlier chapters of this book, she was particularly interested in the chapter on the sacraments, for this was something relatively new to her.

However, we Catholics may not stop at renewing the sacramental side of the healing ministry, for if we did there would still be some things lacking. We have to encourage in general Catholics everywhere to pray more for healing – and to pray with a more expectant faith. And we have to face up to the fact that God wants to give and indeed does give some Christians gifts of healing, a special ministry of praying for healing. It is this last point which seems to be difficult for many Catholics, partly because they tend to identify gifts of healing with sanctity, as I explained in the last chapter. So they think that someone who exercises a ministry of healing prayer is claiming to be a saint! Or they may simply feel threatened by someone exercising a healing ministry.

There is no doubt that Catholics who develop a healing ministry of prayer do tend to run into quite a lot of opposition, especially if their healing ministry is powerful. I myself have been fortunate in this matter. The late Dom Edmund M. Jones OSB, who was my prior for many years, gave me real support in my growing healing ministry, and then my colleagues elected me as prior after his death. In our community we have a tradition of freedom and tolerance. However, I think that women religious who have gifts of healing tend to have a more difficult time, although I know of one sister with a powerful gift of healing whose mother general recommends sick sisters to go to her for healing prayer – and there is the outstanding example of Sr Briege McKenna OSC. It is probably especially difficult for a sister in most contemplative communities to develop a ministry of healing prayer with the laying on of hands, but I know of one abbess who does in fact exercise a powerful healing ministry of this kind, and I know a guest-mistress who frequently prays with her guests. (May I make a plea to mother superiors to be open-minded and not too fearful with regards to this ministry?)

Great gifts of healing do, however, seem to attract strong opposition in the Catholic Church. Father Émilien Tardif, a French-speaking Canadian missionary in the Dominican Republic, describes in his book, *Jesus is Alive* (Inter. Montreal, 1985), some of the opposition he had to face. He had the support of not only his bishop, but also of the episcopal conference. However, the Secretary of State for Health accused him on the television of being a charlatan and misleading the people. Others said that the healing miracles would lead people into witchcraft and spiritism. Others talked of mass hysteria and emotionalism, and suggested that he was insane. The devil certainly does not like the healing ministry of prayer and raises up opposition!

In 1 John 4:1 we read: 'Beloved, do not believe every spirit, but test the spirits to see whether they are of God.' Obviously gifts and ministries of healing need to be tested, as do other gifts. But gifts of healing should be treated in the same open-minded and serene way as gifts of teaching and administration. I fear that in some instances in the Catholic Church gifts of healing are approached with a presupposition that this is almost certainly something false and dangerous which needs to be suppressed. There can also be the attitude of playing-safe-at-any-price. Of course if no one exercises the gift of healing prayer there will be no danger of anything going wrong with it, just as if no one sings in church there is no danger of the singing going wrong. But in both cases there would be a real impoverishment of what should be there.

A further element working against the acceptance of gifts of healing in the Catholic Church is, I think, the influence of secular thought and of unbelief in the Catholic Church today. I also believe that in the ecumenical dialogue some Catholics have been over-influenced by Liberal Protestantism and insufficiently influenced by the Eastern churches, the Evangelicals and the Pentecostals. So some Catholics, including a few priests, despite the official teaching of the Church, would not believe in or at any rate would doubt the historical reality of the healing miracles of Jesus. Obviously if someone does not think that Jesus healed the sick, it is logical not to accept that prayer to Jesus today is doing that very thing. Obviously again, someone taking this view will be very sceptical about the whole healing ministry of prayer, including gifts of healing.

There are some Catholics who would admit that people are being helped and healed in our prayer groups, but they would explain this entirely in psychological terms, not as Jesus or God answering prayer. They would say that the warm, friendly, emotional atmosphere helps some people to feel better, indeed to get better. They might even say that some people have purely natural gifts of healing, which science needs to investigate. But they would refuse to link these gifts with the 'gifts of healing' St Paul wrote about in 1 Corinthians 12. Obviously, an approach which is largely dominated by secularist thought, rationalism and seeing everything in psychological terms is not going to have much time for gifts of healing and the healing ministry of prayer as a whole.

Personally I do not think that God wants to be less generous with his gifts of healing towards Catholics than he is towards Pentecostals and members of other charismatic churches. At the moment, however, these gifts seem to be flourishing much more among these churches than among Catholics. The reason for this is surely that Catholics are in general so much less open to these gifts and to their being exercised in the Christian community. Let us reflect on the words of Cardinal Suenens in his book, *A Controversial Phenomenon. Resting in the Spirit* (Veritas, 1987): 'Christ the Saviour of man is also he who heals man's wounds. His Church has the duty to continue his ministry of healing, to pursue the combat against the Powers of Evil, and to recognize, authenticate and encourage the development of the charism of healing by charting safe roads for it' (page 80).

'And he called the twelve together and gave them power and authority over all demons and to cure diseases, and he sent them out to preach the kingdom of God and to heal' (Luke 9:1). We are increasingly aware in the Catholic Church that many of us have frequently been neglecting the command 'to preach the kingdom of God'. Indeed, one can say, I think, that the Catholic Church is now trying to give top priority to the work of evangelism.

The renewal of the healing ministry is very important from the point of view of the work of evangelism in the Catholic Church. In the quotation from St Luke above, the preaching of the Kingdom of God and the healing in the name of Jesus go together, as they do also in Luke 10: 'Whenever you enter a town and they receive you, eat what is set before you; heal the sick in it and say to them, "The kingdom of God has come near to you" ' (8ff).

Indeed, in the New Testament church we see in practice the preaching of the good news and the healing of the sick going together. 'And they went forth and preached everywhere, while the Lord worked with them and confirmed the message by the signs that attended it. Amen' (Mark 16:20) – the signs being mainly healing, as we can read in the Acts of the Apostles. It is obvious from the Acts of the Apostles that the healing miracles played a key role in the spreading of the gospel and in the early church. To take one example, in Acts 3 we read about the miraculous healing of a man who was lame from birth: seeing this man 'walking and leaping and praising God' the crowd gathered round wanting to know how the miracle had happened; this was the opportunity for Peter to preach the gospel; and 'many of those who heard the word believed; and the numbers of the men came to about five thousand'. Clearly there was a direct link between the healing miracle and the believing of the five thousand: without the healing miracle the crowd would not have been interested in what Peter had to say, and there would have been no five thousand believers.

Indeed, the disciples were so convinced that the preaching and the healing belonged together that they prayed: 'And now, Lord, look upon their threats, and grant to thy servants to speak thy word with all boldness, while thou stretchest out thy hand to heal, and signs and wonders are performed through the name of thy holy servant Jesus' (Acts 4:29). The Lord obviously approved of this prayer, for the text continues: 'And when they had prayed, the place in which they were gathered together was shaken; and they were all filled with the Holy Spirit and spoke the word of God with boldness.'

Does the New Testament practice of closely linking the preaching of the gospel and praying for healing still work in the twentieth century? Well, some Christians have found that it still does. In the Pentecostal churches and in the charismatic fellowships there is a tradition of evangelists with a ministry of healing. If one reads, for instance, the lives of Smith Wiggle-sworth (1859–1947) and Stephen Jeffreys (1876–1943), it is dif-ficult not to believe that they were both used powerfully by God in our own country and elsewhere to heal the sick and to convert many non-believers to Christ. It also seems clear that their evangelism would have been nothing like as successful without the healing dimension (see *Seven Pentecostal Pioneers* by Colin Whittaker, Marshalls, 1983). Or to take the example of someone who is still living and ministering today, Ian Andrews' healing services lead to a considerable number of conversions. I remember him saying once after describing a particularly dramatic physical healing: 'Seventeen people came to Christ as a result of that healing' (see his book: *God can do it Again*, Marshalls, 1982).

Then there is John Wimber and the rapidly expanding Vine-yard Fellowship which he has founded in America. Healings have obviously played an important part in this expansion. Again, there is the example of the German Pentecostal mis-sionary, Reinhard Bonnke, who has been especially active in Africa. A tent which holds 34,000 people has been made for his ministry. At the start of a mission there is often only a small number of people at the front of the tent. But as the news of the healings spread, the tent rapidly fills up on the following evenings. After one campaign of twenty days they planted a new church with a baptized membership of over 600 people. We are now seeing Reinhard Bonnke ministering increasingly often in England, where there are also healings and conversions at his meetings.

Finally, on the Catholic side there is the example of the healing ministry of Monsignor Michael Buckley in this country. His healing services lead not only to many lapsed Catholics coming back to the practice of their religion, but also non-Christians becoming Catholics. Indeed, there have been Mos-lems and Buddhists becoming Catholics as a result of attending his healing services.

However, it is not only a question of evangelists with out-standing healing ministries. In England today the churches which are expanding, and sometimes rapidly, are in general the Pentecostal churches and the charismatic fellowships, while the Catholic Church, along with most other churches, is apparently decreasing in numbers. This is, in my opinion, partly connected with the fact that praying for healing, including physical healing, normally has an important place in the Pentecostal churches and charismatic fellowships, while in the Catholic Church and in general in most other churches it does not.

Jesus promised spiritual power to his disciples: 'But you shall receive power when the Holy Spirit has come upon you; and you shall be my witnesses in Jerusalem and in all Judea and Samaria and to the ends of the earth' (Acts 1:8). I think that an important reason for the lack of growth in many churches and for the weakness of their evangelism is that people do not see or experience much spiritual power in them. Spiritual power is not, of course, only seen in healing miracles, but a truly thriving healing ministry of prayer is a very obvious manifesting of the power of the Holy Spirit. If Christianity is to be considered more than words and people are to believe, then they need to see the power of the Holy Spirit at work in one way or another.

The renewal of the healing ministry of prayer in the Catholic Church, I think, is in the first place a question of fidelity to Jesus, to the New Testament and to the authentic Catholic tradition. However, we can be helped in this fidelity by the example of what the Holy Spirit is doing in other churches. The Decree on Ecumenism of the Second Vatican Council states: 'Nor should we forget that anything wrought by the grace of the Holy Spirit in the hearts of our separated brethren can contribute to our edification. Whatever is truly Christian is never contrary to what genuinely belongs to the faith; indeed, it can always bring a more perfect realization of the very mystery of Christ and the Church' (Chapter 1, number 4). May I suggest that the example of the healing ministry of prayer among Pentecostals and other Christians can contribute to the spiritual renewal of the Catholic Church and to its outreach in evangelism?

Some Catholics may find what I have written here too Pentecostal, too charismatic for their liking. Perhaps it may not be out of place here to quote from Pope John Paul II's address to the International Leaders Conference of Catholic Charismatics on 7 May 1981, quoting Pope Paul VI: 'Pope Paul described the movement for renewal in the Spirit as "A chance for the Church and for the world", and the six years since that Congress have borne out the hope that inspired that vision.' Pope John Paul II also said in that address: 'The priest, for his part, cannot exercise his service on behalf of the Renewal unless and until he adopts a welcoming attitude towards it, based on the desire he shares with every Christian by baptism to grow in the gifts of the Holy Spirit.' However, when I am reflecting upon the renewal of the healing ministry in the Catholic Church I am thinking of something much wider than the Charismatic Renewal, although this movement is, I think, largely spearheading the wider renewal of the healing ministry. One can pray, and pray powerfully, for healing without attending charismatic prayer meetings,

Cardinal Hume has had a few public 'dreams'. Perhaps I may also be permitted to have a 'dream' about the future? I dream of a time, I hope not too far ahead, when there will be praying for healing with the laying on of hands in every Christian family and among Christian friends. I dream of a time when every parish will have its healing team, working with and under the parish clergy. I dream of a time when medical doctors and psychiatrists will send their patients to the parish healing team for prayer, just as the parish healing team refers people to the medical profession. I dream of a time when after Mass on Sunday it will be possible to go forward to have hands laid on for healing prayer for the sickness of spirit, mind or body. I dream of a time when non-Christians will come to the Christian community seeking healing, as they often did in the early church and when the healings that take place will lead to conversions to Christ. I dream of a time when Christians everywhere will have a great devotion to Christ the Healer.

My dream has been strengthened by my annual visits to

Lourdes these last four years, where I have been as the chaplain to charismatic pilgrimages. Lourdes is a place which is very dear to me, for every time I go there my faith in the healing power of Jesus is increased. As I look at the many plaques in the upper basilica giving thanks for healings and as I look at the photographs in the Medical Bureau of the people who have been miraculously healed in Lourdes, I am reminded that praying for healing is an important part of Catholic tradition. So my dream includes the hope that the healing tradition of Lourdes* will spread everywhere among Catholics.

---

*Understandably, many Evangelicals are puzzled by Lourdes where, since Our Lady appeared to St Bernadette in 1858, Jesus has done many healing miracles. Evangelicals may find it interesting to study the history of the healing miracles in Lourdes, where the Medical Bureau makes, I think, a more careful and rigorous scientific examination of alleged cures than any other place in the world. By 1986 2,500 serious cures had been confirmed by the doctors. Anyone wishing further information can write to: Bureau Médical de Notre-Dame de Lourdes, F65100 Lourdes, France. Good books on Lourdes are: *Bernadette of Lourdes*, by René Laurentin (Darton, Longman and Todd, 1979), and *Lourdes. A Modern Pilgrimage*, by Patrick Marnham (Heinemann, 1980).

Epilogue

At the end of this book I realize that I have written nothing or practically nothing about praying for the wider healing: healing disunity in families, in parishes, in neighbourhoods, in countries, between the sexes, classes, races, nations, between divided Christians. Christ's work of redemption can be seen as a great work of healing, in which we are all called to participate. However, it is a mistake to try to cover too much in one book. I will only say that as people become more healed in themselves they will contribute more through prayer and work to the wider healing. Those people who have experienced the healing touch of Jesus in themselves will normally be instruments of healing in the wider world.

My hope and prayer is that this book will encourage and help Christians, especially Catholics, to pray for healing. I hope and pray that some readers will step out in faith with a new confidence in praying for their own healing and that of other people. I hope and pray also that some readers will feel called to a wider ministry of healing prayer. And I also hope and pray that this book will help to curb any exaggerations in the healing ministry.

Members of our prayer groups are praying for those who will read this book – so, dear reader, you have already been prayed for, that the Holy Spirit will be with you in your reading and in your praying for healing. May I invite any readers who feel so called to join with us in our prayer for the renewal of the healing ministry in the Church?

May I make a plea? May I ask readers not to get in touch with me to ask me to pray for their healing? This may seem an ungracious request. But, apart from the fact that there are a considerable number of Christians about who are more gifted than I am in the healing ministry, I am already overwhelmed with requests for healing prayer, and my conscience is already bad enough about the unanswered letters seeking healing ministry which lie on my desk. However, there is also another reason. The whole thrust of this book is to spread the healing ministry, to get more Christians involved in it. So please try praying for healing yourselves, ask your family or Christian friends to pray with you for healing, ask your parish clergy to pray with you, see whether there is a prayer group in your parish or near you and ask them to pray with you, make enquiries as to where suitable Christian healing services are being held in the district where you live.

To help people locate suitable places where they can receive healing prayer, I will give the addresses of two centres in London which have information:

(1) The National Service Committee for Catholic Charismatic Renewal, 484 Kings Road, Chelsea, London, SW10 0LF. Telephone: (01) 352 5298
(2) St Marylebone Centre for Healing and Counselling, St Marylebone Parish Church, Marylebone Road, London, NW1 5LT. Telephone: (01) 935 6374

One final point: some writing on healing would be discredited if the author's health collapsed soon after writing. Not so with this book. The truth of what I have written would not be affected by what may happen to my health. Before this book appears in six months' time I may have died of cancer or a heart attack, I may have gone blind or deaf, I may have contracted Parkinson's disease or multiple sclerosis, or have become paralyzed. Not, I hasten to add, that I am showing signs of a collapse in health. But anybody's health can fail at any time, without anything having gone wrong with God's loving providence – and at the age of sixty-seven no one could be surprised at difficulties with health. However, because I pray for my own health and ask other people to pray for it, I think that in fact it is considerably less likely to collapse than would otherwise be the case. But all that is in the hands of God. 'Your will be done on earth as it is in heaven.'

Against this background of acceptance, let us pray with all our heart, mind and strength, for ourselves and others: 'Come Holy Spirit, with all your healing light and love and power. Amen.'

Testimonies

Introduction

We are two medical doctors who work in Community Medicine as Developmental Paediatricians. Since coming into Charismatic Renewal several years ago, the Lord has taught us that disease is not only healed through medical skills but also through healing prayer. Our work as doctors has been greatly enriched by healing prayer – we see more healing taking place. Doctors, psychiatrists, spiritual counsellors and Christians with the gift of healing prayer all go to make up God's healing team.

Through the healing ministry of prayer, we have experienced at first hand the many and varied ways in which the healing power of Jesus works. Authentic prayer for healing invariably brings into play a supernatural force and the results are often quite striking.

Our experience leads us to the conviction that Jesus still heals people today as he did two thousand years ago. Divine healing does happen – and quite commonly too.

Through the ministry of healing prayer, we have witnessed wonderful cures worked under our very eyes. This has brought us to a deeper awareness that God's healing power can do for us more than any human physician is able to.

Among the wonders we have been privileged to witness are spontaneous regression of tumours, total cures of irreversible disease processes and immediate remission of illnesses known to be incurable by medical means.

Emotional healing is as real as physical healing, in fact, more so. Through prayer we have seen time and time again people freed from long-standing alcoholism, drug abuse and depressive disease.

Doctors today are conscious of the close relationship between mind, spirit and body and that wholeness in these areas is essential for good health. Some of the most dramatic physical healings we have seen have followed deep inner healing of the spirit and the emotions.

The link between diseases like arthritis, ulcerative colitis, gastric ulcers, high blood pressure, heart disease, asthma, migraine and even cancer, with negative emotions is quite generally accepted.

Extraordinary healing of these conditions occurs with some frequency. Through healing prayer, the roots of these illnesses, such as fear, anger, bitterness, resentment and guilt have been healed.

The medical profession may call these 'psychosomatic' cures and, indeed, they may be. But what we must remember is that a psychosomatic cure is a real cure. Many doctors agree that 75–80% of our illnesses are of psychosomatic origin. People with psychosomatic problems are often far more difficult to cure than others. When dealing with physical sickness, at least 75% of our effort should primarily be directed towards the healing of the 'psyche', that is, the emotions. We find that Jesus also heals the psyche and emotions.

The healing testimonies which follow seem to us to be good examples of Jesus healing people in answer to prayer, and we are convinced of the authenticity of these healings. We have added very brief medical notes at the end of many of the testimonies. These healings, however, have not received the official recognition of the Church, which recognition depends on the competent ecclesiastical authorities.

Joseph Briffa MD
Dorothy Briffa MD

Fr James Overton

In February 1969 my back went out of place when I attempted to carry some heavy ladders. One of the lumbar vertebrae was displaced and this caused great pain and discomfort, which lasted until June 1975. At the beginning of this period I was in constant pain and unable to sleep in a normal bed or sit in armchairs. Instead I had to lie on a board and sit on hard chairs. I received medical attention involving wearing a surgical corset, spending two months in a plaster jacket and having traction for several weeks. None of these conventional methods brought any relief. However, a course of treatment under an osteopath in London during 1970 did bring some relief to the severe pain, but there was still considerable pain and I still had to sleep on a board and avoid soft chairs.

In May 1975 I attended a talk given by a Jesuit priest, Father M. S., at The Grail, Pinner, where he spoke about the wounds each of us has received and how, therefore, we should judge each other compassionately. The days following this talk showed me very clearly that I was harbouring much resentment against my parish priest and that I was judging him harshly without taking into account the wounds that had been inflicted upon him and which had affected his personality. I had a clear sense that I needed to go to confession to acknowledge my sin of arrogance, judgement and lack of love, care and compassion towards my parish priest. I sought out Father M. S. and made my confession to him. At the end of the confession he prayed over me for healing of my back. Two nights later when I got on to my board to sleep, I found the pain impossible so I got up, removed the board and slept in a normal bed. During the night I experienced my back moving into place. This was accompanied by a feeling of warmth and a sensation of electricity passing along my back. When I got up the following morning all the pain was gone, and over the next two or three weeks I was conscious of strength moving into my back and of warmth and healing taking place. At the end of this period my back was completely healed.

I did ask for healing prayer for my back several times before 1975, but it was only the clear recognition of sin and true repentance for it that allowed subsequent healing prayer to be effective. I do not believe it was psychosomatic healing because I was not expectant of healing as previous prayer had not been effective. If there had been any expectation the two-day delay certainly destroyed that. I am convinced that this healing was a sovereign intervention from God but that the key element was repentance for my sinful attitudes and judgements.

MEDICAL NOTE: A slipped vertebral disc almost always requires surgical treatment in order to affect a complete cure.

Dr M. Jessudas

I have been a medical practitioner since 1980 and I had no history of any physical illness until June 1986. I then developed a viral flu-like illness. After consultation, I was assured by a specialist that I was suffering from a viral infection which was a self-limiting illness and there was no cause for concern.

As time passed, I started losing weight and my legs progressively became weaker. In August 1986 I was admitted to the Intensive Care Unit of a hospital because of weakness in all four limbs and early breathing difficulty. After investigations, I was found to be suffering from a malignant tumour of the spine. Being a family man with two young children, my first reaction was one of panic. I had never experienced such an emotional crisis. However, being a medical man I had faith in medical science. But, notwithstanding my hopes, I continued to deteriorate even after radiation treatment. As no further treatment was available, after radiation I was sent home and the doctors had given up hope. I lay in the bed paralysed from the waist down and partially paralysed in the arms.

During this most difficult time in my life, I was introduced to a charismatic prayer group in Cockfosters by a family practitioner. Until then, I had simply ignored the power of prayer, although I had always believed in a higher being (God).

One of the women leaders of this charismatic prayer group came to my house with two of the other members and they prayed with me for healing. They laid hands on me and anointed me with the sacramental of blessed oil. The power of Christ was brought to bear on my life.

When during their first visit, they were laying hands on my back and legs, I felt a sensation of warmth in my spine and down my legs. I experienced a strong desire to move my limbs. Although I could not move my legs straightaway, I was able immediately to move my arms with power. This I could not do before.

I was also prayed with for the infilling of the Holy Spirit. When Jesus filled me with his Spirit, from being negative and apprehensive, I became more positive. Healing of mind and soul was accomplished quite dramatically. Although the physical healing was not as sudden as the emotional and spiritual healing, through regular prayer and anointing with blessed oil, I have been improving ever since.

From being totally bedridden I am now free from cancer and able to walk with little difficulty and look after my family. Without the Charismatic Renewal and the group's prayers, I am quite certain that this new chapter of my life would not have taken place. The group prayed over me frequently for six months. The tumour in my back got smaller and smaller until it disappeared and my mobility increased. I am now working full-time as a hospital consultant again.

MEDICAL NOTE: Malignant tumours of the spine where doctors have given up hope, are never cured spontaneously.

Sr Eleanor O'Brien

My lungs had been weak from birth and I suffered from bronchitis frequently. While teaching in London's East End for nine years, my bronchitis worsened. Dr Murphy said my only hope of improvement was to 'export'. I was sent to our community in Turloch, California, in 1957, and for six years I kept reasonably well. However, in 1963 I developed a very serious and rather rare lung disease called 'bronchiectasis'.

This meant that with every chest cold, my lungs would choke with phlegm – I would have to go into hospital, be given oxygen day and night and be put on a breathing machine four times a day.When the specialist examined my lungs with a bronchoscope, he told my mother superior that my lungs were like 'cement' and that nothing could be done for me. Breathing out was extremely painful. I could only sleep sitting upright. This continued for nine years and every year I spent weeks in hospital.

In 1971 I attended a 'Life in the Spirit' Seminar in the Jesuit College of San Francisco University. I was prayed over for the baptism of the Spirit. Jesus became very real in my life, and I became deeply convinced of his personal love for me. The Bible also became alive in a new way.

Between 1971 and 1972 I steadily became worse and I also became depressed. On Pentecost Sunday 1972, reluctantly I attended a prayer meeting in San Francisco. I could not join in the praise. Somebody called my name to be prayed over for healing and I accepted. I was very sceptical. Nothing happened, and in fact I felt worse for the next six months.

My superior encouraged me to take a holiday in Ireland. After seeing my sister, I went to Mount Melleray to visit my brother, Father Athanasius. However, all I could do was to retire to bed. I could hardly sleep, eat or walk. One day I crawled to the loft choir for the Night Office. At the Salve Regina, I managed to stand.

An extraordinary event happened. It seemed as if the whole of heaven was descending like a waterfall. I was being filled from my feet upwards, with love, joy, light, life, music, beauty and tremendous energy. It seemed I could not contain it all. I felt like a child again. I wanted to dance. With full voice I sang the Salve Regina with my brand new lungs.

The next morning with my brother, I climbed the Knock-mealdown Mountains. We sang and we cried. We thanked God for my healing. For the last sixteen years I have exchanged an oxygen cylinder for a twelve-string guitar and a bicycle. I cycle around Dagenham performing full-time parish duties. And I have become involved in the ministry of praying for healing for others. I have been singing the Lord's praises daily and I shall give thanks to the Lord as long as I live.

MEDICAL NOTE: Bronchiectasis is a serious, chronic, progressive, obstructive lung disease which still cannot be cured by medical means.

Margaret Jackson

Due to an accident in 1953, a severe blow to my spine resulted progressively during the following twenty years in daily discomfort, constant pain, interspersed with severe debilitating bouts of pain. Weeks of sleepless nights left me despairing and exhausted. The onset of an attack caused agonising pain to shoot across my back. Frequently losing consciousness I would fall (unless my husband were there to save me). The paralysing pain rendered me unable to move until help arrived. Over a period I attended Barnet, University College and The Royal National Orthopaedic Hospitals for treatment. The onset of severe pain was due to the right lower 'sac' moving further to the right. I was medically retired from British Telecom due to the appalling sick record in 1974 – 'chronic incurable spinal complaint'. In April 1975 I sought private help in Harley Street (Doctor Pattinson) hoping for a fusion to lessen the pain, but X-rays revealed disc damage up to five and six in the lower spine and sciliosis convex to the right (curvature). A fusion operation was impossible as this would cause extra burden on the damaged discs and danger of paralysis, which could result in a wheelchair with no promise that pain would be relieved.

In June 1975, at a prayer group at Christ the King, Cockfosters, I was prayed with for healing by a few lay people, led by two priests and a student Jesuit. A priest placed his hand on my back. I felt a strong sensation of heat in my spine and great peace. I slept soundly that night, the pain had lessened, for the first time in years. I got out of bed unassisted, and to my joy found that I was standing upright. The pain was negligible, being present only in my badly stretched muscles, and by the end of the week had gradually disappeared. Doctor Delmount, my GP, was mystified – he advised me to wait six months to see if it were a permanent improvement before he would send me back to Harley Street. My husband commented that if God in his love had healed me, I would still be healed in six months' time.

In January 1976 I revisited Harley Street. X-rays showed the disc damage was still there, but the convex to the right was no longer present – the pain had disappeared because there was no longer pressure on the nerve centres. Doctor Pattinson said that it was impossible for him to have achieved this result surgically. We explained the nature of the prayer ministry received. He said there was no medical explanation, and fervently wished that healing of this kind could apply to other patients whom he could not humanly help.

I had tried to follow Jesus' teaching in my life, but being aware of my weaknesses, knew that I often failed him. I had heard of God's healing love at Lourdes, and elsewhere, but felt that this must be for especially good people who deserved healing. How could I have been so blind to God's love for us all? I now believe that if we turn to him God meets us at our point of need.

I became involved in praying for the healing of others, always receiving wise counsel from a priest and others in leadership positions, as to the guide-lines. Monday evening and Tuesday afternoon prayer groups at Potters Bar bring people together to worship, praise and thank God and to ask for his healing love when requested. The local GP, Doctor Ciezak, sends people to the groups who are in need and so many, praise God, have been blessed spiritually, mentally and physically – often coming to know God's love for the first time. One lady, healed of terminal cancer five years ago, counsels cancer patients at Mount Vernon Hospital. At first she claimed that she had no education to speak, but her simple witness gives hope to so many who otherwise would have no hope in his love.

Ernest Willey

For several months in 1985–6 I had been losing weight and going to the bathroom three times a night. I also was feeling generally unwell. By August 1986 after several investigations, my specialist diagnosed an enlarged prostate, requiring an operation. I still continued to lose weight. Worse was to follow. I also had an ulcer in the mouth which refused to heal. The doctor suspected cancer. My strength continued to fade.

In 1978 I had been baptised in the Spirit. Following prayer for healing by I. A., well-known for his powerful ministry, I was healed of a hiatus hernia. This inspired me to start an ecumenical prayer group in our house. Many healings happened at these meetings. But to continue my story.

My mouth ulcer spread and I found it more difficult to eat or drink. The doctors considered my ulcer to be very serious and they decided not to operate on my prostate before my mouth was cured. I became progressively weaker, losing more weight and all desire to eat. In September 1986 I became semi-conscious and came close to death.

Many people prayed for my healing. On 29 September 1986, I was admitted to hospital and put on an intravenous drip feed. I slowly regained consciousness. The doctors still expected me to die and they sent me home.

However during November 1986 my spirits began to lift. I became determined to live. I started to pray with great faith for my healing. Every day and night, I would claim my healing, praying verses of faith from the Scriptures, such as: 'By his stripes we are healed.' In the name of Jesus, I took authority over my sickness and I rebuked my infirmity. I pictured myself well again.

In January 1987 I saw my oral specialist, and to his utter amazement he found no trace of my mouth condition. Three weeks later he pronounced me completely cured.

In April 1987 I was prayed over for healing of my prostate. On this occasion I rested in the Spirit. Since my mouth had been healed, I returned to my prostate specialist, hoping to receive treatment. After investigations, he could find no trace of prostate or kidney disease. No operation was needed and I was discharged from hospital. The specialist said I should go home and write a book about my healing. Since then I have become actively engaged in the ministry of praying for the healing of others. To Jesus be the praise, honour and glory.

MEDICAL NOTE: A person who has had a malignant ulcer in the mouth has even today a very small chance of permanent cure. Also, prostate gland enlargement is not cured without active treatment, usually surgical.

Fr Brian O'Sullivan

My own experience of the healing ministry in the Church was totally unexpected. It happened at the Conference Centre of Westminster Cathedral 14 years ago, when I went there on a Sunday to attend a Day of Renewal. About 15 years before this I was involved in a motor accident which left me with a twisted pelvis and consequent pressures on the lower vertebrae of the spine. This caused me more or less constant pain, and this pain became more intense if I had to stand for any length of time, such as during the celebration of Mass. I was also in considerable pain when I had to climb in and out of a car, stand up from a seated position or climb stairs.

When I arrived at the Conference Centre all the chairs were occupied, so having already stood for the celebration of two Masses that morning I then had to stand for a further hour. At the end of the prayer meeting I saw an empty chair in a side room and made for it. I sat down very gratefully, and then to my surprise I was surrounded by a small group of people who asked me if I would like them to pray with me for any purpose. I did not realise that this was a normal feature of that Day of Renewal, namely that prayer for healing was always available in the side room after the large prayer meetings. I told them about the pain I was experiencing and they laid hands on my head and prayed for a few minutes very simply and quietly.

I had no expectation of healing and was certainly not in any kind of heightened emotional mood at the time. In fact, when the priest who was leading the small group asked me how the pain was, it was a moment or two before I realized, to my surprise, that it had stopped. I got to my feet and that would normally have been a painful experience, but this time it wasn't. I bent down to touch my toes, something I had not been able to do without pain for a number of years, I made every possible movement I could think of, and found I had total freedom of movement and not the slightest pain of any kind.

A few minutes later I spotted a flight of stairs and I ran up and down several times just for the sheer joy of being able to do this without pain. Later I got into my car, again without pain, and drove home, where I continued to experience total freedom of movement and absence of pain. From that day to this my back has remained healthy and free from pain. I have occasionally 'put my back out' when doing some violent exercise, but this has always proved to be just a brief temporary problem and I have never again experienced the constant pain and discomfort that I had known for so many years.

This was my introduction to the presence of the healing power of God in the Church today. Since then we have often seen the healing power of Jesus at work in parishes.

MEDICAL NOTE: A longstanding disorder of the spine as described here can never be cured medically as happened spontaneously and quite suddenly in this case.

Eileen

I was born in 1950 in County Donegal, Eire, of Irish Catholic parents. My childhood was happy and my parents gave me much love and security. During my teens and early twenties, I was just a Sunday Christian.

In 1973, I came to England to work and I returned home twice a year to see my family. In 1977 my father was taken ill and died a week later. I was devastated and within a few days of his death, I suffered my first epileptic fit. Soon after, I began to lose control of the amount of alcohol I consumed daily. Within a few months I was going into a bar every night and drinking until I was dead drunk.

Despite medication, my epileptic fits continued for the next seven years, becoming more and more frequent.

In my desperate search for help, I went on pilgrimages to Lourdes, Fatima, Rome and the Holy Land. After each pilgrimage, I would feel a little brighter. I felt there was a glimmer of hope that God would heal me. Yet, my fits continued and I still drank myself silly every night.

After seven years which were like a 'living death', a friend invited me to a healing service at St Joseph's Catholic Church in Highgate. The service consisted of prayer and praise and a sermon which spoke to my heart. I heard that Jesus was alive in his Church and he was still working miracles of healing today. With new hope, I went forward at the end of the service for individual prayer and laying on of hands. A member of the healing ministry team (T.H.) discerned that I needed to offer myself to Jesus and to ask him to send his Holy Spirit to take over my life. I agreed this is what I needed more than anything. So T. H. prayed with me and asked Jesus to renew all the graces and gifts of my baptism and confirmation. I instantly experienced a deep peace and a great joy, which have remained with me for the last twenty-seven months.

From that day, my fits ceased and I was able to drink alcoholic drinks in moderation.

One day I went to the healing service and gave a testimony

of my healing. Six months later I gave up drink for Lent, and I have not had a drink since.

Jesus has become real to me. I am convinced that he loves me and was with me throughout my troubled years. I enjoy great peace and joy and my faith means everything to me. I have received the grace to pray for about eight hours a day. Jesus has truly brought me from death back to life. I go to a charismatic prayer meeting twice a week to thank and praise God for the wonders he has worked for me. Blessed be his Holy Name for ever.

MEDICAL NOTE: A person who has had epilepsy for a number of years is most unlikely to be permanently cured, even with continuing medication.

E. S.

Some years ago I came into Charismatic Renewal accidently through my work as a speech therapist. I was treating a priest, who was recovering from a stroke, and as a result of prayer with the laying on of hands by another priest he made a remarkable recovery. Some weeks later, one Sunday morning when some members of the Westminster Prayer Group were visiting our parish in Cockfosters they noticed that I walked with difficulty into church, and to my embarrassment they asked if they could pray with me for healing. After considerable hesitation I consented – the recovery of the priest being uppermost in my mind.

Twenty-five years before I had injured my back as a result of a fall when I was horse riding. I was sixteen at the time and my parents sought the best orthopaedic opinion. Ten months later after many unsuccessful treatments the surgeon operated and removed a disc from my spine. As a result of surgery my right leg was partially numb, I was unable to feel pinpricks; knee and ankle reflexes were absent. My back continued to be painful. On a few occasions I was re-admitted into hospital for traction and put in plaster. When I married I found hoovering and shopping greatly increased the pain. In the morning I had to roll out of bed because I was unable to sit up, and I had to limber up after a hot bath. My back was gradually becoming more painful as the years went by.

During the prayers that Sunday morning when hands were laid on my back I felt heat, and continued to feel the warmth for about thirty hours. Two days later I sat up in bed for the first time for many years and I was able to hoover and shop without pain. My right leg was fully restored and I could feel pinpricks and all the reflex activity was normal.

This happened in 1976. My back continues to be free from pain and I have been riding again many times. Even more remarkable than my physical healing was my spiritual growth. I wanted to give thanks to God so I decided to go to the weekly prayer meetings. I attended against my will for many months until I realised the benefits I was receiving. I came to know Christ Jesus in a personal way. My whole life altered as I learnt to pray. And after experiencing the healing touch of Jesus myself, I have found myself increasingly involved in the ministry of praying for the healing of other people.

MEDICAL NOTE: A long-standing back injury causing serious disability such as this one can never be cured spontaneously.

Sr Ann Laws OSB

In November 1979 I tripped and broke the top of my right femur. I underwent a hip replacement at the Medway Hospital. The operation was successful. However, later the hip ached and I limped. After three years X-rays showed that the prosthesis was wearing out the socket. The surgeon offered cementing the socket, but I decided to wait.

By 1986 I was having prayer for healing regularly. Prayer was often followed by temporary relief from pain. I felt that complete healing required a miracle. But would God perform it for me? The pain got worse and walking was difficult. With greater faith, I started a Novena (a nine-day period of prayer).

On finishing the Novena, I twisted my hip badly and had to consult a surgeon again in October 1986. The surgeon said that the hip joint was slowly becoming looser. So he would either replace the prosthesis, or I should just accept my bad hip physically, mentally, and spiritually. This gave me food for thought.

A Charismatic Retreat was held at Turvey Abbey. Again I was prayed for, but all I wanted was to accept God's will. Providentially, after ministering to two of my Sisters, E. S. placed her hands on my hip and prayed for healing. I began feeling heat in my hip. I did not realise then that my hip was being healed. Later I rejoined my Community and demonstrated to them how I could kneel and rise unaided, something I could not do before.

Next morning, to my surprise, I was standing perfectly upright, was well-balanced and comfortable. I found I could move my leg in all directions. I ran into the garden. I asked myself: 'Shall I walk or run?' Instead, I began to skip, scattering the path's gravel in all directions.

My hip joint became progressively more stable. Seven months later I went to Bedford Hospital for a check-up. The surgeon said on looking at my X-rays: 'The hip has moved into a new position.' I was going to ask questions, but thought otherwise. God obviously had wrought a miracle. Wonder of wonders, I was able to walk again in the fields, join in liturgical dance and spend autumn afternoons sweeping leaves. My friends, this was much more than healing of a joint. It was a new spiritual awareness. A deeper understanding of God's will where my own will was brought into a sublime harmony with his, bringing wholeness of mind, spirit and body. Alleluia.

MEDICAL NOTE: A 'loose' hip joint is very rarely made stable again except by major surgery.

Una Phelan (26 years old)

I am a midwife in a London hospital having trained in Harlow.

I first started to get psoriasis in my ears in March 1985. It was intermittent and controlled by Hydrocortisone. From March 1986 for the next twelve months I had recurrent ear infections which caused me severe irritation and a lot of discomfort and I was under medical care weekly. My ears would weep and I was partially deaf. My career was at stake because I couldn't hear foetal heartbeats. I would wake up in the night scratching my ears. They constantly got infected and I was on antibiotics as well as the Hydrocortisone.

A concerned friend had a sense that the Lord was telling her that I needed to be prayed over for healing. I rejected this very strongly and when I went to examine why I rejected it, I got Psalm 23 (22). I saw I didn't trust the Lord that he could or would want to heal me. There was a really deep fear that I would not be healed even though I wanted to be. Through Psalm 23 (22) I saw how Jesus Christ trusted his Father throughout his life on earth, his passion and crucifixion and this was the type of faith and trust I needed in God. I also saw how I was living out of my own strength and getting very anxious a lot of the time and that most of my psoriasis was a result of this. This led me to a deep repentance to the Lord for my lack of trust in him and for my fears, and I went to confession before being prayed over for healing in March 1987. The following two weeks I had the most severe of ear infections. During that time I claimed the power of the Lord over the itchiness and also over the lies of Satan telling me I wouldn't be healed. A few weeks later the ears cleared up and since then I have had no ear infections and my psoriasis has not caused me any problems.

On my last appointment in clinic a few weeks ago I was discharged. I was told that my ears were completely clear and that I wouldn't have to come back again. I have stopped all the antibiotics and local applications.

I know the Lord has healed me, but the greatest thing is that he showed me my lack of trust in him and brought me to a deep repentance, and I now know that the Lord has the power to do anything in my life if I have faith and trust in him.

MEDICAL NOTE: Psoriasis is a chronic skin disease, for which even today there is no permanent cure.

Winifred – by a retired GP

Winifred, who was a patient of mine, was sixty-nine years of age when in 1978 a malignant breast tumour was diagnosed at a London teaching hospital; it was found to be moderately differentiated grade 2 carcinoma, and a Patey mastectomy was done. One of the lymph nodes excised was found to be infiltrated with the cancer.

Winifred remained well until in 1982 when, with back pain and shortness of breath, she returned to the hospital. X-rays showed many lung opacities and wedging of T8 vertebra. No histological diagnosis was done, but there was shown to be an increased isotope uptake at the level of the spinal lesion and radiological opinion at the time and on subsequent review was that cancerous growths were present in the lungs and spine.

Tamoxifen, a drug which has been proven to be effective in controlling breast cancers, was given in May 1982, and at this time, Winifred somehow got the message that she had not much longer to live. One of the doctors who was looking after Winifred was also a Catholic nun and was a source of strength to Winifred. It seemed that I had also met this doctor-nun a few years earlier, and from this friendship, Winifred learned of a prayer and healing ministry group led by a priest at a local Catholic church in Cockfosters. Winifred, a determined and courageous person, declared that she wished to attend and receive these healing ministries; she was resolutely determined to fight her illness. I attended these meetings with Winifred and her husband on several occasions, and Winifred's GP, who is also a Christian, came too. On the first occasion Ronald,

Winifred's husband, received the healing ministry too, for an acutely painful arthritic knee; the pain disappeared shortly afterwards.

However at first the combination of Tamoxifen and healing prayers seemed not to help Winifred at all and in a few months, in order to give her husband a rest, she went into a hospice where Catholic nuns looked after her and she was started on Prednisone, also continuing with Tamoxifen. About two weeks later Winifred left the hospice and returned home with an increasing chest problem. The professor of surgery and doctors at the hospital expected her to die soon.

The healing prayers continued and Winifred did not die, but steadily improved and in November 1984, February 1985 and March 1987, her chest X-rays were clear. The hospital notes added an exclamation mark to this in February 1985. Winifred continued to go to those of the prayer meetings she could manage, although due to an arthritic hip, she was practically wheelchair bound. Nevertheless, the doctors were again surprised, for, in March 1987, she was able to walk with a Zimmer frame.

At the hospital check-ups after recovery, Winifred was encouraged and strengthened by the professor of surgery who had faith that healing prayers may help a patient.

Winifred eventually died in September 1987 from pneumonia, five and a half years after she had been expected to die.

Sue Watson (29 years old)

I used to work as a SRN nurse in London, but I had to change my career due to an industrial injury. On 4 August 1983 I dislocated my shoulder lifting a patient. Despite a period of rest followed by physiotherapy, I didn't make any progress. I was eventually diagnosed as having a ripped shoulder capsule with recurrent subluxation of my left shoulder, and I went into hospital for a Bankhart's procedure. I made some progress, but I had to have surgery again as the pin fell out of position.

Whilst in hospital a second time I got a blood clot in my left arm, and in using my other arm a lot I severed the right long thoracic nerve of Bell and ended up with a winged scapula. I was told it probably wouldn't heal.

I came home after three weeks in hospital and woke up one morning with extreme restriction of movement in my spine. As the weeks went by this progressed into my hips, knees, fingers, neck joints and sternum. Although I didn't have any positive blood tests, I was diagnosed as having ankylosing spondylitis on the grounds of present condition, family history of psoriasis and past history of having surgery on my ankles when I was eleven for bilateral ankylosis of those joints.

By January 1985 I was in a lot of pain. I had trouble being able to walk, and following surgery my left shoulder was stiff, weak and restricted in movement. My right shoulder was also very weak, painful, had little movement and was deformed. I had to retire from nursing and was registered disabled. My future held an increase of drugs, deformity, pain and probably psoriasis. I was also a worrier.

I went on a strict vegetarian diet. I began to get prayed over every day and as the days went by the Lord started to reveal to me the fears, worries and anxieties that dominated my life. I seemed periodically to go through a period of depression, feeling I was a failure and couldn't cope. I would feel as if I was going 'mad' and I feared I would end up in a psychiatric hospital. I was prayed over for that fear and deliverance was instantaneous. God told me my future was tied up in Christ and he had a perfect plan for my life.

I didn't believe the Lord could heal my fears and anxieties although I believed that, if he wanted to, he could heal me physically. I asked the Lord to show me he could heal my fears and he gave me Wisdom 19:7–9, 22 and Psalm 66:5. This confirmed to me that he could and would heal me. I had to repent of my lack of belief in him. I went to confession and confessed all my sins, fears and wrong attitudes. From this time the pain in my body gradually decreased and within six months I was quite fit, walking normally, able to do a little sport and able to use my hands again. The significant turning point was clearly acknowledging my sinful attitudes and ways of thinking and bringing these to confession in deep repentance.

I went for a medical assessment two weeks ago, which has been a regular occurrence since the accident at work. I was told I needn't come back again as I was as fit as I would ever get, that I didn't have ankylosing spondylitis as it was a progressive disease and I certainly hadn't progressed. I was told I wouldn't regain any greater range of movement in my left shoulder – I have lost external rotation. However, my right shoulder has healed and my left shoulder is a lot stronger within its range.

MEDICAL NOTE: Ankylosing spondylitis is a progressive disease of the spine for which there is no known permanent cure.

Dr Joe Farrugia

One night some years ago, when I was still in medical practice, I woke up with a painful left foot. I assumed it was due to the way I had been lying or maybe the weight of the bedclothes. I uncovered my foot and tried to go to sleep. The pain got no better, but I noticed the left foot feeling much warmer than the right one. Nevertheless, I was sure this was a transient phenomenon. In no time at all, the pain became excruciating and I soon thought I should have to look at the offending member. What I saw frightened me. All the evidence was there – pain, swelling, heat and redness. In short, a massive infection of the foot, for it was now the size of a large melon. I got out of bed, but I could not put any weight on my left foot. I hobbled around as best as I could and took some aspirin. These had no effect. Eventually, I managed to make it to my car and I took out my emergency night bag. I took two Diconal tablets (a very powerful analgesic and hypnotic) and returned to bed. In time, relief came and with it, sleep. In the morning the pain returned and there was no way I could do the morning surgery.

A colleague agreed to provide cover until a locum could be found. My wife took me to the district hospital where I was admitted on the spot. A whole barrage of investigations was carried out, including X-rays and scanning and a presumptive diagnosis of osteomyelitis was made, without however locating the actual locus of infection. I was in pain, feverish, sedated with pain-killers and under massive antibiotic cover by injection. The day I was admitted to hospital, my wife rang a charismatic friend, E. S., and my name was included in the prayer meeting. That weekend I was anointed by a priest who visited me with E. S. and they both prayed with me for healing. Symptomatically, I was getting better, but I was still far from well.

That night I was awakened by a strong wind as if the building was being buffeted from all sides. There was a feeling of fluttering above the roof, the wind dropped and I fell asleep.

Next morning my temperature dropped to normal. I was pain free and the swelling was much reduced. I felt really at ease. When the night sister came to see me before going off duty, I asked her what sort of night she had with all that wind. She told me she had heard nothing, nor had any of the patients mentioned the wind to her. Time came for the ward round. The consultant physician was delighted and a little puzzled. The intramuscular antibiotics were continued for the full course of three weeks.

Ordinarily, the infection of osteomyelitis responds to treatment slowly and signs and symptoms disappear in a gradual pattern. In my case the response was quite sudden – from full-blown infection to virtual regression. All those who had looked after me, physicians, radiologists, pathologists and orthopaedic surgeons were relieved but somewhat puzzled at the rapid recovery. They did not know that I had had a visitor.

Victor M. Xuereb KCJ OSJ *(66 years old)*

In April 1963, I was at the office in Valletta, when all of a sudden I could not move my right leg. I tried to walk, but it was very painful. I was taken home by one of my clerks, and as soon as I reached home my wife called the doctor. He told me that I had plebothrombosis, so I was confined to bed for twenty-one days. After a month I returned to work. In June 1971 I had posterior wall infarct of the heart. This attack repeated itself four times in a period of three weeks, starting with a vice-like pain in my chest which worked up to my left arm. This pain was always present whenever I exerted myself. On the 16 August 1977 I was admitted at St Luke's Hospital (I.T.U.) suffering from posterior wall infarct. I was discharged from hospital twenty-one days later. Eventually I was certified not fit for work in April 1978. In April 1979 I had pulmonary oedema and an enlarged heart. I was given morphine injections and Tefamine suppositories to ease the coughing, and I was compelled to sleep in the sitting position using a bed rest. Whenever I tried to lie down, I used to drown in my sputum. During the period of my illness I used to have eighteen different pills a day.

In February 1983 Father E. M., a Redemptorist priest from the USA, came to Malta and held a number of healing services at different churches on the island. Huge congregations attended these meetings. I personally attended twice. As a matter of fact, I was praying very hard for my dear wife, who suffers from chronic arthritis – she can hardly walk and is always in pain. I never prayed for myself as I always accepted the will of the Lord, and, praise the Lord, I was completely healed forty-eight hours after the last healing service which was held at Christ the King Church in Paola. Late that night I felt somebody tell me to sleep in the normal way after four years of sleeping in the sitting position and also not to take pills. My wife thought I was going crazy, but I insisted, and, praise God, I had the best normal sleep that night, and continued likewise for two months. Then I decided to call my family doctor to check me. After the check-up I was asked whether I was still the same Victor Xuereb he knew!!

Doctor Robert Farrugia Randon certified that I was completely healed and took me off the pills. A copy of this certificate was sent to the ecclesiastical authorities in Malta for record purposes.

I wish to invite all the faithful to join me in thanking the Good Lord for healing me and making me strong enough to look after my dear wife and give a helping hand to my dear children and their families. Miracles do happen! Deo gratias et Mariae.

MEDICAL NOTE: Severe heart failure with fluid in the lungs following several heart attacks almost invariably leads to near total incapacity and ultimately death.

Vera Norris

My name is Vera Norris, I am 78 years old, and I am a Methodist. I retired on medical grounds at the age of 52 with rheumatoid and osteo-arthritis. Doctors told me I would never walk again. Also, certain medical drugs I had taken had damaged the maculae of my eyes. In 1969, I was registered 'partially sighted' and in 1984, I was registered 'blind'. Five years ago I prayed to die. I was in constant pain. I was angry with God, because I felt utterly useless.

Suddenly, new friends started to come into my life and I began to attend Cockfosters prayer meeting. Here I received tremendous spiritual uplift.

In June 1986, I joined several members of the prayer group on a pilgrimage to Lourdes. Before going there I had had physiotherapy at the North Middlesex Hospital. I was given a stout walking stick and told nothing else could be done for me. By the time of my departure to Lourdes, I was hardly able to lean my weight on my right leg. My balance was gone. The physiotherapist warned me that I was not to walk alone. Provision of a wheelchair was made for me in Lourdes.

One morning, during the Healing Mass in the new hospital chapel in Lourdes, I began to weep copiously. I wept for a long time and I felt that all that was sinful in me had been washed away. My heart was filled with joy. Later on in the day, another pilgrim prophesied to me that what I had just experienced was only the beginning. After lunch we went on a walking tour of Lourdes, but I sat in the wheelchair.

In the Basilica square, the group formed a circle and we prayed for healing, with the laying on of hands. I was left in the wheelchair in the shade of a tree.

Suddenly, I felt a sensation of being lifted up into the air in my chair and this happened three times. I heard a clear voice saying: 'Get up and walk.' But I had not walked unaided for twenty-three years and I was nervous. The voice ordered: 'Ask Joe.' I looked around and I saw Joe (Penfold) in a shaft of sunlight, some distance away. Normally, I would not have been able to see him. At my request Joe came over and helped me to rise from the chair. I stood up, turned round and started to walk slowly and effortlessly. The miracle had happened.

There was much rejoicing, and praising and thanking the Lord that day in Lourdes. My cup was overflowing. For the first time in twenty-three years I was able to kneel down to pray. The Lord had simultaneously restored much of my vision – I was able to distinguish far more details of objects around me and see colours clearly. I can now read my wrist-watch at a normal distance.

Praise the Lord.

MEDICAL NOTE: Degeneration of the macula of the retina causes severe loss of vision, which does not recover. A twenty-three year history of disability due to severe arthritis affecting many joints cannot medically speaking be restored instantly as in this case.

Select Bibliography

Arbuthnot, Andy and Audrey, *Love that Heals*. Marshall Pickering 1986.

Buckley, Michael, *His Healing Touch*. Fount Paperbacks 1987.

DiOrio, Ralph A., *Called to Heal*. Image Books, Doubleday 1984.

Ernest, Johanna, *The Life of Dorothy Kerin*. The Dorothy Kerin Trust, Burrswood, Kent, 1983.

Faricy, Robert, *Praying for Inner Healing*. S.C.M. Press 1979.

Feider, Paul A., *Healing and Suffering: The Christian Paradox*. Darton, Longman and Todd 1988.

Gardner, R. F. R., *Healing Miracles: A Doctor Investigates*. Darton, Longman and Todd 1987.

Kelsey, Morton T., *Healing and Christianity*. S.C.M. Press 1973.

Kuhlman, Kathryn, *I Believe in Miracles*. Lakeland 1963.

Laurentin, René, *Miracles in El Paso?* Servant Publications 1982.

Linn and Linn, Dennis and Matthew, *Healing of Memories*. Paulist Press 1974.

Linn and Linn, Dennis and Matthew, *Healing Life's Hurts*. Paulist Press 1978.

Linn, Linn and Linn, Mary, Dennis and Matthew, *Healing the Dying*. Paulist Press 1979.

Linn and Linn, Dennis and Matthew, *Deliverance Prayer*. Paulist Press 1981.

Linn and Linn, and Fabricant, Matthew, Dennis and Sheila, *Prayer Course for Healing Life's Hurts*. Paulist Press 1983.

Linn, Linn, and Fabricant, Matthew, Dennis and Sheila, *Healing the Greatest Hurt*. Paulist Press 1985.

MacNutt, Francis, *Healing*. Ave Maria Press 1974.

MacNutt, Francis, *The Power to Heal*. Ave Maria Press 1977.

Maddocks, Morris, *The Christian Healing Ministry*. SPCK 1981.

Maddocks, Morris, *Twenty Questions About Healing*. SPCK 1988.

Marnham, Patrick, *Lourdes. A Modern Pilgrimage*. Heinemann 1980.

Monden, Louis, *Signs and Wonders – A Study of the Miraculous Element in Religion*. Desclee Company 1966.

McAll, Kenneth, *Healing the Family Tree*. Sheldon Press, SPCK, 1982.

McBain, Douglas, *Eyes that See: The Spiritual Gift of Discernment*. Marshall Pickering 1986.

McKenna and Libersat, Briege with Henry. *Miracles Do Happen*. Veritas Publications 1987.

McManus, James, *The Ministry of Deliverance in the Catholic Tradition*. National Service Committee for Catholic Charismatic Renewal, 484 Kings Road, London, SW10 0LF, 1980.

McManus, Jim, *The Healing Power of the Sacraments*. Ave Maria Press 1984.

Neil-Smith, Christopher, *The Exorcist and the Possessed*. James Pike Ltd 1974.

Peddie, J. Cameron, *The Forgotten Talent*. Fontana Books 1966.

Perry, Michael, *Deliverance, Psychic Disturbances and Cult Involvement*. SPCK 1987.

Pullinger, Jackie, with Andrew Quicke, *Chasing the Dragon*. Hodder and Stoughton 1980.

Pytches, David, *Come Holy Spirit: Learning how to Minister in Power*. Hodder and Stoughton 1985.

Richards, John, *But Deliver Us From Evil*. Darton, Longman and Todd 1974.

Richards, John, *The Question of Healing Services* Daybreak/Darton, Longman and Todd 1989.

Sanford, Agnes, *Healing Gifts of the Spirit*. Arthur James 1949.

Scanlan, Michael, *The Power in Penance: Confession and the Holy Spirit*. Ave Maria Press 1972.

Shlemon, Barbara Leahy, *Healing Prayer*. Ave Maria Press 1976.

Shlemon, Linn and Linn, Barbara Leahy, Dennis and Matthew, *To Heal as Jesus Healed*. Ave Maria Press 1978.

Shlemon, Barbara Leahy, *Healing the Hidden Self*. Ave Maria Press 1982.

Suenens, Léon-Joseph, *Renewal and the Powers of Darkness*. Darton, Longman and Todd 1983.

Sullivan, Francis A., *Charisms and Charismatic Renewal*. Gill and Macmillan 1982.

Tardif, Émilien, José H. Prado Flores, *Jesus is Alive*. Éditions Inter, Montreal, 1985.

Thomas, Leo, *The Healing Team – a practical guide for effective ministry*. Paulist Press 1987.

Wallis, Arthur, *God's Chosen Fast – a spiritual and practical guide to fasting*. Victory Press 1968.

Whittaker, Colin, *Seven Pentecostal Pioneers*. Marshall, Morgan and Scott 1983.

Wimber, John, with Kevin Springer, *Power Healing*. Hodder and Stoughton 1986.